LET'S SPEAK
PHRASEBOOK
OF
MANDARIN
CHINESE

外国人学说
中国话

五洲传播出版社

FOREWORD
Qiányán （前言）

PART1 Basic Words & Expressions
Jīběn Jùxíng （基本句型）[010-043]

PART2　Making Introductions
Jièshào（介绍）[044-059]

PART3　Accommodations
Zhùsù（住宿）[060-073]

PART4　Going out
Chūxíng（出行）[074-099]

PART5　Eating out
Wàichū Jiùcān（外出就餐）[100-121]

PART6 Shopping
Gòuwù（购物）［122–137］

Appendix
Fùlù（附录）[174-191]

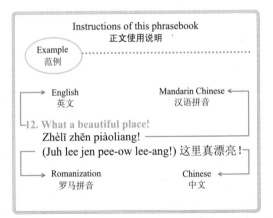

Instructions of this phrasebook
正文使用说明

Example
范例

English
英文

Mandarin Chinese
汉语拼音

12. What a beautiful place!

Zhèlǐ zhēn piàoliang!

(Juh lee jen pee-ow lee-ang!) 这里真漂亮！

Romanization
罗马拼音

Chinese
中文

FOREWORD
Qiányán （前言）

Mandarin Chinese
Hànyǔ Pīnyīn （汉语拼音）

Hanyu Pinyin (汉语拼音), commonly called Pinyin, is the most common variant of Standard Mandarin in use. *Hanyu* means the Chinese language, *pin* means "spell" and *yin* means "sound". Pinyin uses Roman letters to represent sounds in Standard Mandarin, however, they are pronounced differently. The pronunciation of Chinese is generally given in terms of initials and finals.

b (as in **b**oy)	**g** (as in **g**irl)	**zh** (as in ju**dg**e)
p (as in **p**ark)	**k** (as in **k**id)	**ch** (as in **ch**urch)
m (as in **m**ay)	**h** (as in **h**at)	**sh** (as in **sh**ow)
f (as in **f**orum)	**j** (as in **j**eep)	**r** (as in **r**ubber)
d (as in **d**og)	**q** (as in **ch**eese)	**z** (as in rea**ds**)
t (as in **t**ime)	**x** (as in **sh**eep)	**c** (as in ca**ts**)
n (as in **n**urse)	**w** (as in **w**ay)	**s** (as in **s**ay)
l (as in **l**ove)	**y** (as in **y**es)	

a (as in f**a**ther)	**ai** (as in b**uy**)	**ie** (as in y**es**)
o (as in m**o**rning)	**ei** (as in **eigh**t)	**üe** (German ü+ye)
e (as in g**i**rl)	**ui** (as in w**ai**t)	**er** (as in w**or**ld)
i (as in s**ee**)	**ao** (as in n**ow**)	**an** (as in **un**der)
u (as in b**oo**t)	**ou** (as in l**ow**)	**en** (as in wom**en**)
ü (as in French tu or German Fühlen)	**iu** (as **you**)	**in** (as in **in**)

un (as in we**nt**)	**ong** (as in s**ong**)	**ua** (as in w**aft**)
ün (as in German grü**n**)	**ia** (as in **Asia**)	**uai** (as in w**ife**)
	ian (as in Austral**ian**)	**uan** (as in **one**)
ang (as in l**ung**)	**iang** (as in **young**)	**uang** (u+ang)
eng (as in wome**n+ng**)	**iao** (as in m**eow**)	**uo** (as in w**ar**)
ing (as in th**ing**)	**iong** (i+long)	

Tones are an important part of Chinese. They are the variation of pitch within a syllable and are used to distinguish words with the same Pinyin. There are basically four tones plus a neutral tone in Mandarin Chinese. Each tone is represented by a diacritical mark above a non-medial vowel. The neutral tone is uesd for stressless syllables and its pitch is determined by the tones of adjacent syllables. N. B. a neutral is never a starting tone.

Tones	Tone Marks	Descriptions	Examples
1st tone	–	Flat or High Level Tone (阴平)	Mā（妈） Bā（八）
2nd tone	´	Rising or High-Rising Tone (阳平)	Má（麻） Bá（拔）
3rd tone	ˇ	Falling-Rising or Low Tone (上声)	Mǎ（马） Bǎ（把）
4th tone	`	Falling or High-Falling Tone (去声)	Mà（骂） Bà（爸）
neutral tone	No mark or dot before syllable	Neutral Tone (轻声)	Ma（吗） Ba（吧）

Basic Words & Expressions
Jīběn Jùxíng (Gee Ben Jew Shing)
基本句型

Greetings Wènhòu (When Hoh) 问候

I Questions

1. **How are you?**
   Nǐ hǎo ma? (Knee how ma?) 你好吗？

2. **How are you doing? / How is it going?**
   How's everything with you? / How have you been?
   Zuìjìn zěnmeyàng? (tz-way qin 'tz'-en muh yang?)
   最近怎么样？

3. **How have you been recently?**
   Zuìjìn shēntǐ hái hǎo ma? ('tz'-way qin shen tee hi how ma?) 最近身体还好吗？

4. **How's your family?**
   Nǐ de jiārén hǎo ma? (Knee duh gee-ah ren how ma?)
   你的家人好吗？

5. **How was your …?**
   … zěnmeyàng? (… 'tz'-en muh yang?)

... 怎么样？

* vacation/ holiday	jiàqī (gee-ah chee) 假期
* weekend	zhōumò (joe moh-uh) 周末

6. What's happening?

Jìnlái hǎo ma? (Qin lie how ma?) 近来好吗？

7. What's new?

Jìnkuàng rúhé? (Qin 'qu'-ang roo huh?)
近况如何？

8. Why are you in such a good / bad mood?

Nǐ zěnme xīnqíng zhème (bù) hǎo?
(Knee 'tz'-en muh shin ching juh muh (boo) how?)
你怎么心情这么(不)好？

9. Is anything wrong?

Yǒu shénme bù duìjìn ma? (Yoh shen muh boo 'd'
-way qin ma?) 有什么不对劲吗？

* I / me	wǒ (wuh) 我
* he (him) / she (her)	tā (ta) 他/她
* we / us	wǒmen (wuh men) 我们
* you (pl)	nǐmen (knee men) 你们
* they / them	tāmen (ta men) 他们
* you	nǐ (knee) 你
* mine	wǒ de (wuh duh) 我的

Let's
speak
phrasebook
of mandarin
Chinese

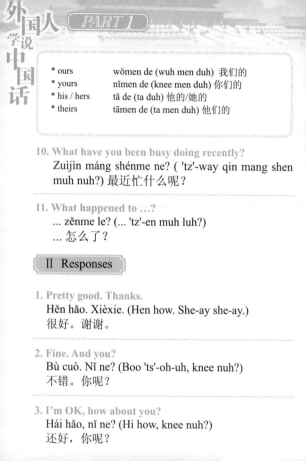

* ours	wǒmen de (wuh men duh) 我们的
* yours	nǐmen de (knee men duh) 你们的
* his / hers	tā de (ta duh) 他的/她的
* theirs	tāmen de (ta men duh) 他们的

10. What have you been busy doing recently?

Zuìjìn máng shénme ne? ('tz'-way qin mang shen muh nuh?) 最近忙什么呢？

11. What happened to …?

… zěnme le? (… 'tz'-en muh luh?)
… 怎么了？

II Responses

1. Pretty good. Thanks.

Hěn hǎo. Xièxie. (Hen how. She-ay she-ay.)
很好。谢谢。

2. Fine. And you?

Bù cuò. Nǐ ne? (Boo 'ts'-oh-uh, knee nuh?)
不错。你呢？

3. I'm OK, how about you?

Hái hǎo, nǐ ne? (Hi how, knee nuh?)
还好，你呢？

4. **Not bad.**
Bù cuò. (Boo 'ts'-oh-uh.) 不错。

5. **Just so so.**
Yībān. ('e' ban.) 一般。

6. **So far so good.**
Dào mùqián hái hǎo. (Dow moo chee-an hi how.)
到目前还好。

Ⅲ Small Talk

1. **Hi / hello!**
Nǐ hǎo! (Knee how!) 你好！

2. **How do you do! (To seniors or superiors to show respect)**
Nín hǎo! (Nin how!) 您好！

3. **Good morning / afternoon / evening / night!**
Zǎoshang hǎo! (Tzow shang how!) 早上好！
Xiàwǔ hǎo! (She-ah woo how!) 下午好！
Wǎnshang hǎo! (Wan shang how!) 晚上好！
Wǎn'ān! (Wan an!) 晚安！

4. **Long time no see.**
Hǎojiǔ bù jiàn. (How gee-oh boo gee-an.)
好久不见。

Let's
speak
phrasebook
of mandarin
Chinese

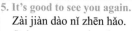

5. It's good to see you again.

Zài jiàn dào nǐ zhēn hǎo.

('tz'-eye gee-an dow knee jen how.) 再见到你真好。

6. I haven't seen much of you lately.

Wǒ jìnlái bù cháng jiàn dào nǐ. (Wuh qin lie boo chang gee-an dow knee.) 我近来不常见到你。

7. You're a sight for sore eyes.

Jiàn dào nǐ zhēn hǎo.

(Gee-an dow knee jen how.) 见到你真好。

8. Please give my best regards to your parents.

Qǐng dài wǒ xiàng nǐ fùmǔ wènhǎo.

(Ching die wuh she-ang knee foo moo when how.)
请代我向你父母问好。

TIPS

"你" is used among the peers and friends, while "您" is used to show respect to the elder people or those of higher work status.

Chinese way of greeting

Chinese greetings always revolve around points of situation and actions with regards to target persons. These are considered a little private and cannot be asked casually by westerners. E.g.,

1. Have you had your meal? (Usually around the meal time)

   Chīle ma? (Chur luh ma?) 吃了吗？

2. Are your going out? (When you are going out)

   Chūqù ya? (Chew chew yah?) 出去呀？

Saying Goodbye
Gàobié (Gow Bee-eh) 告别

1. **Goodbye!**
   Zàijiàn! ('tz'-eye gee-an!) 再见！

2. **So long.**
   Gàocí le. (Gow 'ts'-uh luh.) 告辞了。

3. **Hope to see you again.**
   Hòu huì yǒu qī.
   (Hoh hui yoh chee.) 后会有期。

Goodbye! Zàijiàn!

4. **Take care.**
   Duō bǎozhòng.
   (Doh-uh bow zhong!) 多保重！

5. **See you ...**

   * in a little while
   Yīhuìr jiàn. ('e' hui gee-an.) 一会儿见。

   * later
   Huítóu jiàn. (Hui toe gee-an.) 回头见。

   * tomorrow
   Míngtiān jiàn. (Ming tee-an gee-an.) 明天见。

   * next week
   Xià xīngqī jiàn. (She-ah shing chee gee-an.) 下星期见。

Let's
speak
phrasebook
of mandarin
Chinese

6. I will call you when I arrive.

Dàole yǐhòu wǒ gěi nǐ dǎ diànhuà.

(Dow luh 'e' hoh wuh gay knee da dee-an hwa.)

到了以后我给你打电话。

---

7. Let's keep in touch!

Jīngcháng liánxì a! (Jing chang lee-an she a!)

经常联系啊!

---

8. Here's my ...

Zhè shì wǒ de ... (Juh sure wuh duh ...)

这是我的 ...

* phone   diànhuà (dee-an hwa) 电话
* address dìzhǐ (dee jur) 地址
* email   yóuxiāng (yoh she-ang) 邮箱
* card   míngpiàn (ming pee-an) 名片

Here is my card.
Zhè shì wǒ de míngpiàn.

Saying Thanks Gǎnxiè (Gan She-ay) 感谢

I General

1. Thank you.
   Xièxie. (She-ay she-ay.)
   谢谢。

---

2. Thank you very much!
   Fēicháng gǎnxiè! / Duō xiè!
   (Fay chang gan she-ay! / Doh-uh She-ay!)
   非常感谢！/ 多谢！

---

3. Thanks for your help.
   Xièxie nǐ de bāngzhù.
   (She-ay she-ay knee duh bang zhu.)
   谢谢你的帮助。

---

4. Thank you for all your hard work.
   Xīnkǔle, xièxie nín.
   (Shin koo luh, She-ay she-ay nin.)
   辛苦了，谢谢您。

---

5. We are really sorry for troubling you.
   Gěi nín tiān máfan le, zhēn bù hǎoyìsi.

Let's
speak
phrasebook
of mandarin
Chinese

(Gay nin tee-an ma fan luh, jen boo how 'e' si.)

给您添麻烦了，真不好意思。

II Responses

1. **You're welcome. / Not at all.**
Bùyòng xiè. (Boo yong she-ay.)
不用谢。

3. **Don't mention it. / Never mind.**
Bù kèqi. (Boo kuh chee.)
不客气。

5. **You're quite welcome.**
Nǐ tài kèqi le. (Knee tye kuh chee luh.)
你太客气了。

6. **It's nothing.**
Méi shénme ! (May shen muh!)
没什么！

7. **It doesn't matter.**
Méi guānxi. (May gu-on she.)
没关系。

Apologies & Forgiveness
Dàoqiàn hé Yuánliàng (Dow Chee-an Huh You-an Lee-ang) 道歉和原谅

I General

1. **I'm sorry (I apologize).**
   Duìbuqǐ / Bàoqiàn / Bù hǎoyìsi.
   ('d' -way boo chee / Bow chee-an / Boo how 'e' si.)
   对不起 / 抱歉 / 不好意思。

2. **I'm really sorry!**
   Zhēn duìbuqǐ! (Jen 'd' -way boo chee!) 真对不起！

3. **I didn't mean to.**
   Wǒ bù shì gùyì de. (Wuh boo sure goo 'e' duh.)
   我不是故意的。

4. **Please forgive me.**
   Qǐng yuánliàng. (Ching you-an lee-ang.) 请原谅。

5. **Sorry, I am late.**
   Fēicháng bàoqiàn, wǒ lái wǎn le. (Fay chang bow chee-an, wuh lie wan luh!) 非常抱歉，我来晚了。

6. **I'm sorry to have kept you waiting.**
   Duìbuqǐ, ràng nín jiǔděng le. ('d' -way boo chee,

Let's speak phrasebook of mandarin Chinese

PART 1

rang nin gee-oh deng luh.) 对不起，让您久等了！

II Responses

1. **No problem.**
Méi wèntí. (May when tee.) 没问题。

2. **Never mind. / That's all right.**
Méi guānxi. (May gu-on she.) 没关系。

3. **It's OK.**
Méi shìr / Bù yào jǐn. (May sure. / Boo yow qin.)
没事儿 / 不要紧。

4. **Forget it.**
Suàn le. (Sue-an luh.) 算了。

5. **It's not your fault.**
Bù shì nǐ de cuò. (Boo sure knee duh 'ts'-oh-uh.)
不是你的错。

Compliment & Appreciation
Zànyáng hé Xīnshǎng
(Tz'-an Yang Huh Shin Shang) 赞扬和欣赏

1. **Great / Excellent!**
Bàng jí le! (Bang gee luh!) 棒极了！

2. Wonderful!

Tài hǎo le! (Tye how luh!) 太好了！

3. You are great!

Nǐ zhēn bàng! (Knee jen bang!) 你真棒！

4. You are so charming!

Nǐ zhēn piàoliang! (Knee jen pee-ow lee-ang!)
你真漂亮！

5. Beijingers are very kind-hearted!

Běijīngrén zhēn hǎo! (Bay jing ren jen how!)
北京人真好！

6. Beijing is such a large city!

Běijīng tài dà le! (Bay jing tye da luh!)
北京太大了！

7. Beijing is better than we imagined!

Běijīng bǐ wǒmen xiǎngxiàng de hǎo!
(Bay jing bee wuh men she-ang she-ang duh how!)
北京比我们想象的好！

8. You are really remarkable!

Nǐ zhēn liǎobùqǐ! (Knee jen lee-ow boo chee!)
你真了不起！

9. Well done!

Let's
speak
phrasebook
of mandarin
Chinese

Nǐ zuò de hěn hǎo.
(Knee 'z'-oh-uh duh hen how.) 你做得很好。

10. You are truly a good man!

Nǐ zhēn shì gè hǎorén!
(Knee jen sure guh how ren!) 你真是个好人！

11. You sing so well!

Nǐ chàng de zhēn hǎotīng. (Knee chang duh jen how ting!) 你唱得真好听！

12. What a beautiful place!

Zhèlǐ zhēn piàoliang!
(Juh lee jen pee-ow lee-ang!) 这里真漂亮！

TIPS

Chinese way of responding to others' compliment

Chinese people are usually very modest and when being praised, they always say things like "哪里哪里", "过奖了", "还差得远呢" instead of directly saying "谢谢". E.g.,

1. That's nothing. / It's not at all.
   Nǎlǐ nǎlǐ. (Na lee na lee.) 哪里哪里。
2. You are flat me.
   Nín guò jiǎng le. (Nin goh-uh gee-ang luh.) 您过奖了。
3. It's not that great.
   Hái chà de yuǎn ne. (Hi chah duh you-an nuh.)
   还差得远呢。

Blaming & Complaining
Zébèi hé Bàoyuàn
(Tzuh Bay Huh Bow You-an) 责备和抱怨

1. **The traffic is very heavy in Beijing!**
Běijīng chē tài duō le!
(Bay jing chuh tye doh-uh luh!)
北京车太多了!

2. **There are so many people in Beijing!**
Běijīngrén tài duō le!
(Bay jing ren tye doh-uh luh!)
北京人太多了!

3. **I'm afraid I have a complaint to make about the service.**
Wǒ duì nǐmen de fúwù yǒu yìjiàn.
(Wuh 'd'-way knee men duh foo woo yoh 'e' gee-an.)
我对你们的服务有意见。

4. **You ought to be ashamed of ...**
Nǐ yīng wèi ... gǎndào xiūkuì.
(Knee ying way ... gan dow she-oh 'k'-way.)
你应为 ... 感到羞愧。

5. **Why on earth did you say such a silly thing to me?**
Nǐ duì wǒ shuō zhèzhǒng huà jiūjìng shì shénme

Let's
speak
phrasebook
of mandarin
Chinese

yìsi? (Knee 'd'-way wuh show-uh juh zhong hwa gee-oh jing sure shen muh 'e' si?)
你对我说这种话究竟是什么意思?

---

6. **You have no right to help yourself!**

Nǐ wú quán zìjǐ dòngshǒu! (Knee woo chew-an 'tz'-uh gee dong show!) 你无权自己动手!

---

7. **I'm not at all satisfied with ...**

Wǒ duì ... yīdiǎnr yě bù mǎnyì.
(Wuh 'd'-way ... 'e' dee-an yeh boo man 'e'.)
我对 ... 一点儿也不满意。

---

8. **You ought to be more careful next time.**

Nǐ xià cì zài bù néng zhèyàng cūxīn le. (Knee she-ah 'ts'-uh 'tz'-eye boo neng juh yang 'ts'-oh-uh shin luh.)
你下次再不能这样粗心了。

---

9. **I get very annoyed about it.**

Wǒ duì cǐ fán tòu le. (Wuh 'd'-way 'ts'-uh fan toe luh.) 我对此烦透了。

---

10. **Can't you be serious for once?**

Nǐ jiù bù néng yánsù yī cì? (Knee gee-oh boo neng yan soo 'e' 'ts'-uh?) 你就不能严肃一次?

---

11. **Please, mind your own business.**

Qǐng bié gānshè wǒ de sīshì. (Ching bee-eh gan

shuh wuh duh si sure.) 请别干涉我的私事。

---

12. **It's not nice of you to behave like that.**
Nǐ nàyàng zuò tài bù xiànghuà le.
(Knee na yang 'z'-oh-uh tye boo she-ang hwa luh.)
你那样做太不像话了。

Surprise & Being Puzzled
Jīngyà hé Yíhuò (Jing Yah Huh 'e' Huo)
惊讶和疑惑

---

1. **Oh, my god!**
A ya! (A yah!) 啊呀！

---

2. **Wow!**
Wa! (Wah!) 哇！

I can't believe it!
Jiǎnzhí ràng rén wúfǎ xiāngxìn!

---

3. **Really!**
Zhēn de ma?
(Jen duh ma?) 真的吗？

---

4. **How strange!**
Zhēn qíguài!
(Jen chee gu-eye!) 真奇怪！

---

5. **Not really!**
Bù huì ba! (Boo hui ba!) 不会吧！

---

6. What? You don't know this.

Shénme? Nǐ jìngrán bù zhīdào? (Shen muh? Knee jing ran boo jur dow?) 什么？你竟然不知道？

7. I can't believe it!

Jiǎnzhí ràng rén wúfǎ xiāngxìn! (Gee-an jur rang ren woo fa she-ang shin!) 简直让人无法相信！

8. Incredible!

Bù kě sī yì! (Boo kuh si 'e'!) 不可思议！

9. Surely not!

Zěnme néng zhèyàng!
('tz'-en muh neng juh yang!) 怎么能这样！

Approval & Disapproval
Zànchéng hé Fǎnduì
('tz'-an Chung Huh Fan 'd'-way) 赞成和反对

1. OK.
Hǎo de. (How duh.) 好的。

2. Alright.
Kěyǐ. (Kuh 'e'.) 可以。

3. Exactly.
Duì. ('d'-way.) 对。

4. **That's right.**

Méi cuò. (May 'ts'-oh-uh.) 没错。

---

5. **That's OK with me.**

Xíng a. (Shing a.) 行啊。

---

6. **No problem.**

Méi wèntí. (May when tee.) 没问题。

---

7. **I agree.**

Wǒ tóngyì. (Wuh tong 'e'.) 我同意。

---

8. **I think so, too.**

Wǒ yě zhème rènwéi. (Wuh yeh juh muh ren way.)
我也这么认为。

---

9. **That's a good idea!**

Zhēn shì gè hǎo zhǔyi! (Jen sure guh how jew 'e'!)
真是个好主意！

---

10. **You have a point there.**

Nǐ shuō de yǒu dàolǐ. (Knee show-uh duh yoh dow lee.) 你说得有道理。

---

11. **No!**

Bù xíng. (Boo shing.) 不行。

---

12. **No way!**

Jué bù / Méi ménr! (Jew-ay boo / May men!)

决不 / 没门儿！

---

13. **It makes no sense.**

Zhè méi dàolǐ. (Juh may dow lee.) 这没道理。

---

14. **I disagree with you.**

Wǒ bù tóngyì nǐ de yìjiàn.

(Wuh boo tong 'e' knee duh 'e' chee-an.)
我不同意你的意见。

---

15. **I don't think so.**

Wǒ bù zhème rènwéi.

(Wuh boo juh muh ren way.) 我不这么认为。

Expressing Good Wishes & Congratulations
Zhùfú (Joe-uh Foo) 祝福

---

1. **Congratulations!**

Gōngxǐ nǐ! (Gong she knee!) 恭喜你！

---

2. **Congratulations on your marriage!**

Zhù nǐmen xīnhūn kuàilè!

(Joe-uh knee men shin hun kwai luh!)
祝你们新婚快乐！

---

3. **Congratulations for your good fortune!**

Gōngxǐ fācái!

(traditional Chinese New Year's future use)
(Gong she fa 'ts'-eye!) 恭喜发财!

---

4. Enjoy your vacation!

Jiàrì yúkuài! (Gee-ah ree you kwai!) 假日愉快!

---

5. Let's drink to ...

Wèi ... gānbēi! (Way ... gan bay!) 为 ...干杯!

Happy Birthday!
Shēngrì kuàilè!

---

7. Good luck!

Zhù nǐ hǎoyùn!
(Joe-uh knee how yun!)
祝你好运!

---

6. Every success in your new job!

Zhù nǐ xīn gōngzuò shùnlì!
(Joe-uh knee shin gong 'z'-oh-uh shun lee!)
祝你新工作顺利!

---

8. Happy Birthday / New Year / Spring Festival!

Shēngrì / Xīnnián / Xīnchūn kuàilè!
(Sheng ree / Shin knee-an / Shin chun kwai luh!)
生日 / 新年/ 新春快乐!

---

9. Have a nice trip!

Lǚtú yúkuài!
(Lü too you kwai!) 旅途愉快!

Let's
speak
phrasebook
of mandarin
Chinese

10. I hope you are successful!

Zhù nǐ chénggōng! (Joe-uh knee chung gong!)

祝你成功！

11. Merry Christmas!

Shèngdàn kuàilè! (Sheng dan kwai luh!)

圣诞快乐！

12. I wish you a happy life and long lasting marriage!

Zhù nǐmen xìngfú, báitóudàolǎo!

(Koe-uh knee men shing foo, buy toe dow low!)

祝你们幸福，白头到老！

13. I wish you a healthy life / lucky New Year!

Zhù nǐ shēntǐ jiànkāng / láinián dàjí! (Joe-uh knee shen tee chee-an kang / lie knee-an da gee!)

祝你身体健康 / 来年大吉！

14. I wish you a life of happiness and prosperity!

Wànshìrúyì! (Wan sure roo 'e'!) 万事如意！

Numbers Shùzì (Shoe 'tz'-uh) 数字

* 0	líng (ling) 〇 / 零		* 3	sān (san) 三 / 叁
* 1	yī ('e') 一 / 壹		* 4	sì (si) 四 / 肆
* 2	èr (are) 二 / 贰		* 5	wǔ (woo) 五 / 伍

* 6 ...... liù (lee-oh) 六 / 陆
* 7 ...... qī (chee) 七 / 柒
* 8 ...... bā (ba) 八 / 捌
* 9 ...... jiǔ (gee-oh) 九 / 玖
*10 ...... shí (sure) 十 / 拾

* 11 ...... shíyī (sure 'e') 十一
* 20 ...... èrshí (are sure) 二十
* 21 ...... èrshíyī (are sure 'e') 二十一
* 100 ..... yībǎi ('e' buy) 一百
* 101 ..... yībǎi líng yī ('e' buy ling 'e') 一百零一
* 123 ...... yībǎi èrshísān ('e' buy are sure san) 一百二十三
* 200 ...... èrbǎi (are buy) 二百
* 1,000 ...... yīqiān ('e' chee-an) 一千
* 10,000 ...... yīwàn ('e' wan) 一万
* 100,000 ...... shíwàn (sure wan) 十万
* 1,000,000 ...... yībǎi wàn ('e' buy wan) 一百万

* 1st ...... dì-yī (dee 'e') 第一
* 2nd ...... dì-èr (dee are) 第二
* 3rd ...... dì-sān (dee san) 第三
* 4th ...... dì-sì (dee si) 第四
* 5th ...... dì-wǔ (dee woo) 第五
* 6th ...... dì-liù (dee lee-oh) 第六
* 7th ...... dì-qī (dee chee) 第七
* 8th ...... dì-bā (dee ba) 第八
* 9th ...... dì-jiǔ (dee gee-oh) 第九
* 10th ...... dì-shí (dee sure) 第十

Let's
speak
phrasebook
of mandarin
Chinese

Time & Date
Shíjiān hé Rìqī (Sure Gee-an Huh Ree Chee)
时间和日期

Time   Shíjiān (Sure Gee-an) 时间

* o'clock	diǎn (dee-an)	点
* hour	xiǎoshí (she-ow)	小时
* minute	fēnzhōng (fen zhong)	分钟
* second	miǎo (meow)	秒
* quarter	kè (kuh)	刻
* half	bàn (ban)	半

Week   Xīngqī (Shing Chee) 星期

* Monday	xīngqīyī (shing chee 'e')	星期一
* Tuesday	xīngqīèr (shing chee are)	星期二
* Wednesday	xīngqīsān (shing chee san)	星期三
* Thursday	xīngqīsì (shing chee si)	星期四
* Friday	xīngqīwǔ (shing chee woo)	星期五
* Saturday	xīngqīliù (shing chee lee-oh)	星期六
* Sunday	xīngqīrì (shing chee ree)	星期日

1. What time is it now?

Xiànzài jǐ diǎn le? (She-an 'tz'-eye gee dee-an luh?)
现在几点了？

2. It's ... now.

Xiànzài ... le. (She-an 'tz'-eye ... luh.) 现在 ... 了。

* six o'clock   liù diǎn (Lee-oh dee-an) 六点
* a quarter to six
    chà yīkè liù diǎn
    (Cha 'e' kuh lee-oh dee-an) 差一刻六点

3. **How long do you need to …?**

Nǐ xūyào duō cháng shíjiān ...? (Knee shoe yow doh-uh chang sure gee-an ...?) 你需要多长时间 ...?

4. **How soon…?**

Duōjiǔ yǐhòu ...? (Doh-uh gee-oh 'e' hou ...?)
多久以后 ...?

5. **My watch is five minutes fast / slow.**

Wǒ de biǎo kuài / màn wǔ fēnzhōng.
(Wuh duh bee-ow kwai / man woo fen zhong.)
我的表快 /慢五分钟。

6. **Let's meet at 4:25 tomorrow afternoon.**

Jiù dìng míngtiān xiàwǔ sì diǎn èrshíwǔ fēn ba.
(Gee-oh ding ming tee-an she-ah woo si dee-an are sure woo fen ba.) 就定明天下午4点25分吧。

7. **What day is today?**

Jīntiān xīngqī jǐ? (Gin tee-an shing chee gee?)
今天星期几?

8. **What day is it today?**

Jīntiān shì jǐ yuè jǐ hào? (Gin tee-an sure gee you-eh

gee how?) 今天是几月几号？

---

9. Today is August 8, 2008.

Jīntiān shì liǎngqiān líng bā nián bā yuè bā hào.

(Gin tee-an sure lee-ang chee-an ling ba knee-an ba you-eh ba how.) 今天是2008年8月8号。

---

10. When did you start to work?

Nǐ nǎ yī nián cānjiā gōngzuò de?

(Knee na 'e' knee-an 'ts'-an gee-ah gong 'z'-oh-uh duh?) 你哪一年参加工作的？

	Month Yuè (You-eh) 月
* January	yī yuè ('e' you-eh) 一月
* February	èr yuè (are you-eh) 二月
* March	sān yuè (san you-eh) 三月
* April	sì yuè (si you-eh) 四月
* May	wǔ yuè (woo you-eh) 五月
* June	liù yuè (lee-oh you-eh) 六月
* July	qī yuè (chee you-eh) 七月
* August	bā yuè (ba you-eh) 八月
* September	jiǔ yuè (gee-oh you-eh) 九月
* October	shí yuè (sure you-eh) 十月
* November	shí yī yuè (sure 'e' you-eh) 十一月
* December	shí èr yuè (sure are you-eh) 十二月

The Weather & Seasons
Tiānqì hé Jìjié (Tee-an Chee Huh Gee Gee-ay) 天气和季节

1. **What a fine day today!**

Jīntiān tiānqì zhēn hǎo a! (Gin tee-an tee-an chee jen how a!) 今天天气真好啊！

2. **It's likely to rain soon.**

Guò yīhuìr kěndìng huì xiàyǔ. (Go-uh 'e' hui ken ding hui she-ah you.) 过一会儿肯定会下雨。

3. **If it is fine tomorrow, I want to go shopping.**

Rúguǒ míngtiān tiānqì hǎo, wǒ jiù qù mǎi dōngxi. (Roo go-uh ming tee-an tee-an chee how, wuh gee-oh chew my dong she.) 如果明天天气好，我就去买东西。

4. **It will soon be ...**

... mǎshàng lái le. (... ma shang lie luh.) ... 马上来了。

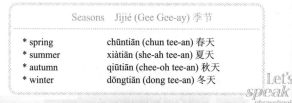

Seasons	Jìjié (Gee Gee-ay) 季节	
* spring	chūntiān (chun tee-an)	春天
* summer	xiàtiān (she-ah tee-an)	夏天
* autumn	qiūtiān (chee-oh tee-an)	秋天
* winter	dōngtiān (dong tee-an)	冬天

Let's
speak
phrasebook
of mandarin
Chinese

5. How will the weather be for the next few days?

Wèilái jǐ tiān de tiānqì zěnmeyàng?

(Way lie gee tee-an duh tee-an chee 'tz'-en muh yang?) 未来几天的天气怎么样？

Weather & Climate　Tiānqì hé Qìhòu
(Tee-an Chee Hur Chee Hou) 天气和气候

* sunny　　　qínglǎng de (ching lang duh) 晴朗的
* windy　　　yǒu fēng de (yoh feng duh) 有风的
* cloudy　　　duōyún de (doh-uh yun duh) 多云的
* foggy　　　yǒu wù de (yoh woo duh) 有雾的
* cold　　　　hánlěng (han leng) 寒冷
* warm　　　wēnnuǎn (when new-an) 温暖
* hot　　　　rè (ruh) 热
* damp　　　cháoshī (chow sure) 潮湿
* dry　　　　gānhàn (gan han) 干旱

Weather Forecast　Tiānqì Yùbào
(Tee-an Chee You Bow) 天气预报

* wind　　　　fēng (feng) 风
* breeze　　　wēifēng (way feng) 微风
* typhoon　　táifēng (tye feng) 台风
* cloud　　　yún (yun) 云
* rain　　　　yǔ (you) 雨
* raining　　　xiàyǔ (she-ah you) 下雨
* shower　　　zhènyǔ (jen you) 阵雨
* downpour　bàoyǔ (bao you) 暴雨
* storm　　　bàofēngyǔ (bao feng you) 暴风雨
* thunder　　léi (lei) 雷

* lightning   shǎndiàn (shan dee-an) 闪电
* snow   xuě (shoe-ay) 雪
* snowfall   jiàngxuě (gee-ang shoe-ay) 降雪
* fog   wù (woo) 雾
* hail   bīngbáo (bing bao) 冰雹
* frost   shuāng (shoe-ang) 霜
* dew   lùshuǐ (lu 'sh'-way) 露水
* freeze   bīngdòng (bing dong) 冰冻

It will soon be winter.
Dōngtiān mǎshàng lái le.

Renminbi (RMB)
Rénmínbì (Ren Min Bi) 人民币

The Renminbi or the *yuan* (元, formal form 圆) is the official currency in the People's Republic of China (PRC). The base unit of the Renminbi is the *yuan*. One *yuan* is divided into 10 *jiao* (角), and one *jiao* is subdivided into 10 *fen* (分). The largest denomination of the Renminbi is the 100-*yuan* note. The smallest is the 1-*fen* coin or note.

China now uses the fifth series of the paper currency, which

Let's
speak
phrasebook
of mandarin
Chinese

was issued in the following denominations: 100 *yuan*, 50 *yuan*, 20 *yuan*, 10 *yuan*, 5 *yuan*, 1 *yuan*; the coins include 1 *yuan*, 5 *jiao* and 1 *jiao*.

* *yuan*	yuán (you-an) 元 / 圓	
* *jiao*	jiǎo (gee-ow) 角	
* *fen*	fēn (fen) 分	
* 1.23 *yuan*	yīyuán èrjiǎo sānfēn	
	('e' you-an are gee-ow san fen) 一元二角三分	
* 100 *yuan*	yìbǎi yuán ('e' buy you-an) 一百元 / 壹佰圓	
* 50 *yuan*	wǔshí yuán (woo sure you-an) 五十元 / 伍拾圓	
* 20 *yuan*	èrshí yuán (are sure you-an) 二十元 / 貳拾圓	
* 10 *yuan*	shí yuán (sure you-an) 十元 / 拾圓	
* 5 *yuan*	wǔ yuán (woo you-an) 五元 / 伍圓	
* 1 *yuan*	yī yuán ('e' you-an) 一元 / 壹圓	
* 5 *jiao*	wǔ jiǎo (woo gee-ow) 五角 / 伍角	
* 1 *jiao*	yī jiǎo ('e' gee-ow) 一角 / 壹角	

Measurements
Jìliàng Dānwèi (Gee Lee-ang Dan Way)
计量单位

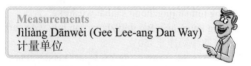

1. The room is five meters long and three meters wide.
   Zhè jiān wūzi yǒu wǔ mǐ cháng, sān mǐ kuān.
   (Juh gee-an woo 'tz'-uh yoh woo me chang, san me kuan.) 这间屋子有5米长，3米宽。

2. I'm 1.82 meters tall.

Wǒ shēngāo yī mǐ bā èr.

(Wuh shen gao 'e' me ba are.) 我身高一米八二。

3. **My house is about 90 square meters.**

Wǒ jiā dàgài yǒu jiǔshí píngmǐ. (Wuh gee-ah da guy yoh gee-oh sure ping me.) 我家大概有90平米。

4. **The Summer Palace covers an area of 290 hectares.**

Yíhéyuán zǒngmiànjī èrbǎi jiǔshí gōngqǐng. ('e' huh you-an 'tz'-ong me-an gee are buy gee-oh sure gong ching.) 颐和园总面积290公顷。

5. **These apples weigh about 2 *jin*.**

Zhèxiē píngguǒ dàgài yǒu liǎng jīn. (Juh she-ay ping go-uh da guy yoh lee-ang gin.) 这些苹果大概有两斤。

6. **The net weight of this bottle of milk is 350 grams.**

Zhè píng niúnǎi jìngzhòng sānbǎi wǔshí kè. (Juh ping knee-oh 'n'eye jing zhong san buy woo sure kuh.) 这瓶牛奶净重350克。

7. **You are restricted to eight liters of duty-free wine.**

Xiédài de miǎnshuì jiǔ bù dé chāoguò bā shēng. (She-ay die duh me-an 'sh'-way gee-oh boo duh chow go-uh ba sheng.) 携带的免税酒不得超过8升。

Let's
speak
phrasebook
of mandarin
Chinese

* kilometer	gōnglǐ / qiānmǐ (gong lee/ chee-an me) 公里 / 千米	
* meter	mǐ / gōngchǐ (me/ gong chur) 米 / 公尺	
* decimeter	fēnmǐ (fen me) 分米	
* centimeter	límǐ (lee me) 厘米	
* millimeter	háomǐ (how me) 毫米	
* hectare	gōngqǐng (gong ching) 公顷	
* square	píngfāng (ping fong) 平方	
* cube	lìfāng (lee fong) 立方	
* liter	gōngshēng / shēng (gong sheng /sheng) 公升/ 升	
* ton	dūn (dun) 吨	
* kilogram	gōngjīn / qiānkè (gong gin / chee-an kuh) 公斤 / 千克	
* gram	kè (kuh) 克	
* *chi*	chǐ (chur) 尺	
* *cun*	cùn ('ts'-un) 寸	
* *liang*	liǎng (lee-ang) 两	
* *mu*	mǔ (moo) 亩	
	1 *mu* = 666.7 square meters	
	(1 moo = 666.7 ping fong me)	
* *zhang*	zhàng ('j'-ang) 丈	
	1 *zhang* = 10 *chi* = 100 *cun* = 3.33 meters	
	(1 'j'-ang = 10 chur = 100 'ts'-un = 3.33 me)	
* *jin*	jīn (gin) 斤	
	1 *jin* = 10 *liang* = 500 grams	
	(1 gin = 10 lee-ang = 500 kuh)	

Emergencies
Tūfā Shìjiàn (Too Fa Sure Gee-an)
突发事件

1. **Help!**
   Jiùmìng a! (Gee-oh ming a!) 救命啊！

2. **Fire!**
   Zháohuǒ la! ('j' - ow huo la!) 着火啦！

3. **Stop thief!**
   Zhuā xiǎotōu! (Jew-ah she-ow toe!) 抓小偷！

4. **Can you help me?**
   Nǐ néng bāngzhù wǒ ma?
   (Knee neng bang jew wuh ma?) 你能帮助我吗？

5. **Somebody helps me!**
   Kuài lái rén a! (Kwai lie ren a!) 快来人啊！

Let's
speak
phrasebook
of mandarin
Chinese

6. Please do me a favor.

Qǐng bāngbang wǒ. / Bāng wǒ yī xià.

(Ching bang bang wuh. / Bang wuh 'e' she-ah.)

请帮帮我。/ 帮我一下。

---

7. Please give me a hand.

Qǐng nín bāng ge máng. (Ching nin bang guh mang.)

请您帮个忙。

---

8. Can you direct me to the …? / Can you tell me the way to the …?

Nǐ néng gàosù wǒ qù … zěnme zǒu ma? (Knee neng gao sue wuh chew …'tz'-en muh tzoh ma?)

你能告诉我去 … 怎么走吗?

* police office	jǐngchájú (jing chah jew) 警察局
* hospital	yīyuàn ('e' you-an) 医院

---

9. I've been robbed.

Wǒ bèi qiǎng le. (Wuh bay chee-ang luh.) 我被抢了。

---

10. My wallet was stolen.

Wǒ de qiánbāo bèi tōu le. (Wuh duh chee-an bow bay toe luh.) 我的钱包被偷了。

---

11. His injuries are severe.

Tā shāngshì hěn yánzhòng.

(Ta shang sure hen yan zhong.) 他伤势很严重。

12. He can't breathe.

Tā hūxī kùnnán. (Ta who she 'k'uhn nan.)

他呼吸困难。

13. We must phone for an ambulance.

Wǒmen děi dǎ diànhuà jiào jiùhùchē le.

(Wuh men duh da dee-an hwa gee-ow gee-oh who chuh luh.) 我们得打电话叫救护车了。

14. There is a traffic accident up ahead.

Qiánmiàn chū jiāotōng shìgù le.

(Chee-an me-an chew gee-ow tong sure goo luh.)

前面出交通事故了。

15. I lost my … and I want to go to the police office to make a certification on lost.

Wǒ de … diū le. Wǒ xiǎng dào pàichūsuǒ kāi diūshī zhèngmíng.

(Wuh duh ... dee-oh luh, wuh she-ang dow pie chew sew- uh 'k'-eye dee-oh sure jung ming.)

我的 … 丢了，我想到派出所开丢失证明。

Emergency Phone Numbers	
110	Police
119	Fire
120	First-Aid Center
122	Traffic Police
999	Emergency Services

Let's speak *phrasebook* of mandarin *Chinese*

Making Introductions
Jièshào (Gee-ay Sh-ow) 介绍

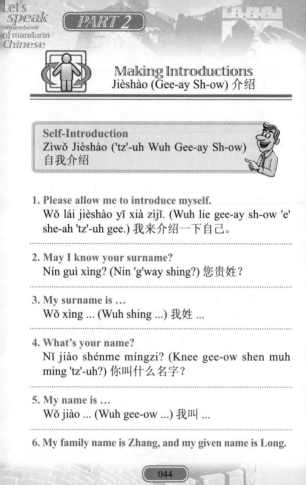

Self-Introduction
Zìwǒ Jièshào ('tz'-uh Wuh Gee-ay Sh-ow)
自我介绍

1. **Please allow me to introduce myself.**
Wǒ lái jièshào yī xià zìjǐ. (Wuh lie gee-ay sh-ow 'e' she-ah 'tz'-uh gee.) 我来介绍一下自己。

2. **May I know your surname?**
Nín guì xìng? (Nin 'g'way shing?) 您贵姓？

3. **My surname is …**
Wǒ xìng ... (Wuh shing ...) 我姓 ...

4. **What's your name?**
Nǐ jiào shénme míngzi? (Knee gee-ow shen muh ming 'tz'-uh?) 你叫什么名字？

5. **My name is …**
Wǒ jiào ... (Wuh gee-ow ...) 我叫 ...

6. **My family name is Zhang, and my given name is Long.**

Wǒ xìng Zhāng, jiào Zhāng Lóng.
(Wuh shing 'j'-ang, gee-ow 'j'-ang long.)
我姓张，叫张龙。

---

7. This is Miss Tang.

Zhè wèi shì Táng xiǎojiě.

(Juh way sure tang she-ow gee-ay.) 这位是唐小姐。

Titles	Chēnghū (Chung Who) 称呼
* Mr.	xiānsheng (she-an sheng) 先生
* Madam	nǚshì (nü sure) 女士
* Miss	xiǎojiě (she-ow gee-ay) 小姐

8. She is Li Hong.

Tā shì Lǐ Hóng. (Ta sure lee hong.) 她是李红。

---

9. Let me introduce Wang Ming to you.

Wǒ lái jièshào yī xià. Zhè wèi shì Wáng Míng.

(Wuh lie gee-ay sh-ow 'e' she-ah. Juh way sure wang ming.) 我来介绍一下。这位是王明。

---

10. Nice to meet you.

Hěn gāoxìng rènshi nǐ.

(Hen gao shing ren sure knee.) 很高兴认识你。

---

11. I've heard a lot about you.

Jiǔyǎng dàmíng.

外国人说中国话

PART 2

(Gee-oh yang da ming.) 久仰大名。

TIPS

A Chinese name consists of two parts, beginning with the surname and is then followed by the given name. And when Chinese address each other, they usually add the title or the position after the surname to show their respect, e.g., "王先生""李小姐" etc. As in western countries: to call someone by his or her given name is only to show intimacy.

Nationality & Language
Guójí hé Yǔyán (Go-uh Gee Huh You Yan)
国籍和语言

1. **What's your nationality?**
   Nǐ shì nǎ guó rén?
   (Knee sure na go-uh ren?) 你是哪国人？

2. **I am a(n) ...**
   Wǒ shì ... (Wuh sure ...) 我是 ...

* Chinese	Zhōngguórén (zhong go-uh ren)	中国人
* American	Měiguórén (may go-uh ren)	美国人
* British	Yīngguórén (ying go-uh ren)	英国人
* Canadian	Jiānádàrén (gee-ah na da ren)	加拿大人
* Australian	Àodàlìyàrén (ow da lee yah ren)	
		澳大利亚人

* French	Fǎguórén (fah go-uh ren)	法国人
* German	Déguórén (duh go-uh ren)	德国人
* Spanish	Xībānyárén (she ban yah ren)	西班牙人
* Italian	Yìdàlìrén ('e' da lee ren)	意大利人
* Russian	Éluósīrén (are low-uh si ren)	俄罗斯人
* South Korean	Hánguórén (han go-uh ren)	韩国人
* Japanese	Rìběnrén (ree ben ren)	日本人

3. Where are you from?

Nǐ cóng nǎlǐ lái? (Knee 'ts'-ong na lee lie?)

你从哪里来?

---

4. I'm from …

Wǒ lái zì … (Wuh lie 'tz'-uh …) 我来自…

---

5. I was born in …

Wǒ shì zài … chūshēng de. (Wuh sure 'tz'-eye … chew sheng duh.) 我是在 … 出生的。

* China	Zhōngguó (zhong go-uh)	中国
* Beijing	Běijīng (bay jing)	北京
* Shanghai	Shànghǎi (shang hi)	上海
* Guangzhou	Guǎngzhōu ('g'wang joe)	广州
* Xi'an	Xī'ān (she an)	西安
* Tianjin	Tiānjīn (tee-an gin)	天津
* Hong Kong	Xiānggǎng (she-ang gang)	香港
* Macao	Àomén (ow men)	澳门
* Taiwan	Táiwān (tye wan)	台湾

外国人学说中国话

Let's
speak
phrasebook
of mandarin
Chinese

PART 2

* the USA	Měiguó (may go-uh)	美国
* Britain	Yīngguó (ying go-uh)	英国
* Canada	Jiānádà (gee-ah na da)	加拿大
* Australia	Àodàliyà (ow da lee yah)	澳大利亚
* France	Fǎguó (fah go-uh)	法国
* Germany	Déguó (duh go-uh)	德国
* Spain	Xībānyá (she ban yah)	西班牙
* Italy	Yìdàlì ('e' da lee)	意大利
* Russia	Éluósī (are low-uh si)	俄罗斯
* South Korea	Hánguó (han go-uh)	韩国
* Japan	Rìběn (ree ben)	日本

6. Do you speak …?

Nǐ huì shuō ...? (Knee hui show-uh ...?) 你会说 ...?

7. I can speak …

wǒ néng shuō .... (Wuh neng show-uh ...) 我能说 ...

* Chinese	Hànyǔ (han you)	汉语
* English	Yīngyǔ (ying you)	英语
* French	Fǎyǔ (fah you)	法语
* German	Déyǔ (duh you)	德语
* Spanish	Xībānyáyǔ (she ban yah you)	西班牙语
* Italian	Yìdàliyǔ ('e' da lee you)	意大利语
* Russian	Éyǔ (are you)	俄语
* Korean	Hánguóyǔ (han go-uh you)	韩国语
* Japanese	Rìyǔ (ree you)	日语

Professions Zhíyè (Jur Yeh) 职业

1. What do you do?

Nǐ shì zuò shénme gōngzuò de?

(Knee sure 'z'-oh-uh shen muh gong 'z'-oh-uh duh?)

你是做什么工作的？

2. I am a teacher.

Wǒ shì yī míng jiàoshī.

(Wuh sure 'e' ming gee-ow sure.) 我是一名教师。

3. Where do you work?

Nǐ zài nǎr gōngzuò?

(Knee 'tz'-eye na gong 'z'-oh-uh?) 你在哪儿工作？

* doctor	yīshēng ('e' sheng)	医生
* nurse	hùshi (who sure)	护士
* police	jǐngchá (jing chah)	警察
* serviceman	jūnrén (jun ren)	军人
* lawyer	lǜshī (lü sure)	律师
* worker	gōngrén (gong ren)	工人
* farmer	nóngmín (nong min)	农民
* staff member	zhíyuán (jur you-an)	职员
* manager	jīnglǐ (jing lee)	经理
* secretary	mìshū (me shoe)	秘书
* teacher	jiàoshī (gee-ow sure)	教师

外国人学说中国话

PART 2

* student	xuéshēng (shoe-ay sheng)	学生
* businessman	shāngrén (shang ren)	商人
* engineer	gōngchéngshī (gong chung sure)	工程师
* waiter / waitress	fúwùyuán (foo woo you-an)	服务员
* salesperson	xiāoshòuyuán (she-ow show you-an) 销售员	
* civil servant	gōngwùyuán (gong woo you-an)	公务员
* journalist	jìzhě (ge juh)	记者
* scientist	kēxuéjiā (kuh shoe-ay gee-ah)	科学家
* writer	zuòjiā ('z'-oh-uh gee-ah)	作家
* painter	huàjiā (hwa gee-ah)	画家
* artist	yìshùjiā ('e' shoe gee-ah)	艺术家
* musician	yīnyuèjiā (yin you-eh gee-ah)	音乐家
* housewife	jiātíng zhǔfù (gee-ah ting joe-uh foo) 家庭主妇	

---

4. I work in Microsoft.

Wǒ zài wēiruǎngōngsī gōngzuò.

(Wuh 'tz'-eye way roo-an gong si gong 'z'-oh-uh.)

我在微软公司工作。

....

5. I want to have a part-time job.

Wǒ xiǎng zhǎo yī fèn jiānzhí gōngzuò.

(Wuh she-ang 'j'-ow 'e' fen gee-an jur gong 'z'-oh-uh.) 我想找一份兼职工作。

....

6. I've been working for five years.

Wǒ yǐjīng gōngzuò wǔ nián le. (Wuh 'e' jing gong

'z'-oh-uh woo knee-an luh.) 我已经工作五年了。

---

7. When do you go to work?

Nǐmen jǐ diǎn shàngbān?

(Knee men gee dee-an shang ban?)

你们几点上班?

---

8. We usually knock off at about five o'clock.

Wǒmen tōngcháng xiàwǔ wǔ diǎn xiàbān.

(Wuh men tong chang she-ah woo woo dee-an she-ah ban.)

我们通常下午5点下班。

---

9. When do you normally get in from work?

Nǐ píngshí xiàbān jǐ diǎn dàojiā?

(Knee ping sure she-ah ban gee dee-an dow gee-ah?)

你平时下班几点到家?

PART 2

Family & Marriage
Jiātíng hé Hūnyīn (Gee-ah Ting Hur Hun Yin) 家庭和婚姻

1. **How many people are there in your family?**
   Nǐ jiā yǒu jǐ kǒu rén?
   (Knee gee-ah yoh gee koh ren?) 你家有几口人？

2. **There are five people in my family.**
   Wǒ jiā lǐ yǒu wǔ kǒu rén. (Wuh gee-ah lee yoh woo koh ren.) 我家里有五口人。

3. **Do you have any brothers or sisters?**
   Nǐ yǒu xiōngdìjiěmèi ma? (Knee yoh she-ong dee gee-ay may ma?) 你有兄弟姐妹吗？

4. **Are you married?**
   Nǐ jiéhūn le ma?
   (Knee gee-ay hun luh ma?) 你结婚了吗？

5. **I am married.**
   Wǒ jiéhūn le. (Wuh gee-ay hun luh.) 我结婚了。

6. **No, I am not married. I am single.**
   Méi yǒu, wǒ méi jiéhūn. Wǒ dānshēn.
   (May yoh, wuh may gee-ay hun. Wuh dan shen.)
   没有，我没结婚。我单身。

* grandfather	yéye (yeh yeh) 爷爷	
	(father's father)	
* grandfather	lǎoye (low yeh) 姥爷	
	(mother's father)	
* father	bàba (ba ba) 爸爸	
* father-in-law	gōnggong (gong gong) 公公	
	(husband's father)	
* father-in-law	yuèfù (you-eh foo) 岳父	
	(wife's father)	
* husband	zhàngfū ('j'-ang foo) 丈夫	
* uncle	bóbo (boh-uh boh-uh) 伯伯	
	(father's elder brother)	
* uncle	shūshu (shoe shoe) 叔叔	
	(father's younger brother)	
* uncle	jiùjiu (gee-oh gee-oh) 舅舅	
	(mother's brother)	
* elder brother	gēge (guh guh) 哥哥	
* younger brother	dìdi (dee dee) 弟弟	
* son	érzi (are 'tz'-uh) 儿子	
* son-in-law	nǚxu (nü shoe) 女婿	
	(daughter's husband)	
* grandson	sūnzi (sun 'tz'-uh) 孙子	
	(son's son)	
* grandson	wàisūnzi (why sun 'tz'-uh) 外孙子	
	(daughter's son)	
* grandmother	nǎinai ('n'eye 'n'eye) 奶奶	
	(father's mother)	
* grandmother	lǎolao (low low) 姥姥	
	(mother's mother)	
* mother	māma (ma ma) 妈妈	

外国人学说中国话

Let's
speak
phrasebook
of mandarin
Chinese

PART 2

* mother-in-law	pópo (poh-uh poh-uh) 婆婆 (husband's mother)	
* mother-in-law	yuèmǔ (you-eh moo) 岳母 (wife's mother)	
* wife	qīzǐ (chee 'tz'-uh) 妻子	
* aunt	gūgu (goo goo) 姑姑 (father's sister)	
* aunt	yí ('e') 姨 (mother's sister)	
* elder sister	jiějie (gee-ay gee-ay) 姐姐	
* younger sister	mèimei (may may) 妹妹	
* daughter	nǚer (nü are) 女儿	
* daughter-in-law	érxí (are she) 儿媳 (son's wife)	
* granddaughter	sūnnǚ (sun nü) 孙女 (son's daughter)	
* granddaughter	wàisūnnǚ (why sun nü) 外孙女 (daughter's daughter)	

7. **We've just got engaged.**
Wǒmen gānggāng dìnghūn.
(Wuh men gang gang ding hun.)
我们刚刚订婚。

8. **I heard that you're getting married. Congratulations.**
Tīngshuō nǐ yào jiéhūn le, gōngxǐ!
(Ting show-uh knee yow gee-ay hun luh, gong she!)
听说你要结婚了，恭喜！

9. Do you have children?

Nǐ yǒu háizi ma? (Knee yoh hi 'tz'-uh ma?)

你有孩子吗？

10. I have two children, a boy and a girl.

Wǒ yǒu liǎng gè háizi, yī gè nán háir, yī gè nǔ háir.
(Wuh yoh lee-ang guh hi 'tz'-uh, 'e' guh nan hi, 'e'
guh nü hi.)

我有两个孩子，一个男孩儿，一个女孩儿。

TIPS

Generally, westerners don't talk about their personal affairs which are
considered private; therefore it might be considered to be impolite to ask
them about their age, marriage, family, salary, etc. They don't generally
like such inquiry and would feel uncomfortable answering. Thus, such
affairs should be avoided in conversation.

Hobbies
Xìngqù hé Àihào (Shing Chew Huh Eye How)
兴趣和爱好

1. Do you have any hobbies?

Nǐ yǒu shénme àihào?
(Knee yoh shen muh eye how?)

你有什么爱好？

Let's
speak
phrasebook
of mandarin
Chinese

2. One of my hobbies is painting.

Wǒ de àihào zhī yī shì huàhuar.

(Wuh duh eye how jur 'e' sure hwa hwa.)

我的爱好之一是画画儿。

---

3. I'm an amateur photographer.

Wǒ shì gè yèyú shèyǐng àihàozhě.

(Wuh sure guh yeh you shoe ying eye how juh.)

我是个业余摄影爱好者。

---

4. He has a bent for art.

Tā àihào yìshù.

(Ta eye how 'e' shoe.) 他爱好艺术。

---

5. What kind of … do you like?

Nǐ xǐhuan shénmeyàng de …? (Knee she huan shen muh yang duh …?) 你喜欢什么样的 …?

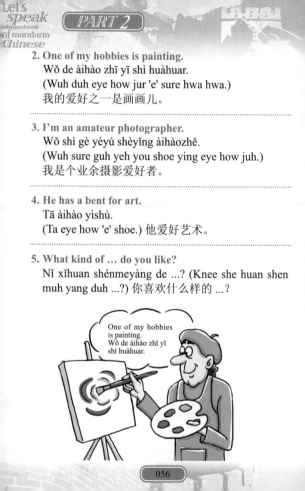

One of my hobbies
is painting.
Wǒ de àihào zhī yī
shì huàhuar.

6. I like ... best.

Wǒ zuì xǐhuan ... (Wuh 'tz'-way she huan ...)

我最喜欢 ...

* music
  yīnyuè (yin you-eh) 音乐
* sports
  yùndòng (yun dong) 运动
* game
  yóuxì (yoh she) 游戏
* TV shows
  diànshìjù (dee-an sure jew) 电视剧
* Kungfu
  gōngfu (gong foo) 功夫
* travel
  lǚyóu (yoh yong) 旅游
* body-building
  jiànshēn (gee-an shen) 健身
* photography
  shèyǐng (shuh ying) 摄影
* swimming
  yóuyǒng (yoh yong) 游泳
* cooking
  pēngrèn (peng ren) 烹饪
* reading
  dúshū (do shoe) 读书
* shopping
  gòuwù (goh woo) 购物
* mahjong
  májiàng (ma gee-ang) 麻将

外国人学说中国话

Let's
speak
phrasebook
of mandarin
Chinese

* playing cards
  dǎ pái (da pie) 打牌
* Chinese shadowboxing
  tàijíquán (tye gee chew-an) 太极拳
* martial arts
  wǔshù (woo shoe) 武术
* playing basketball
  dǎ lánqiú (da lan chee-oh) 打篮球
* playing ping-pong
  dǎ pīngpāngqiú (da ping pang chee-oh) 打乒乓球
* watching movies
  kàn diànyǐng (can dee-an ying) 看电影

Religions
Zōngjiào Xìnyǎng
('tz'-ong Gee-ow Shin Yang) 宗教信仰

1. **What's your religion?**
   Nǐ de zōngjiào xìnyǎng shì shénme?
   (Knee duh 'tz'-ong gee-ow shin yang sure shen muh?)
   你的宗教信仰是什么？

2. **I have no religious beliefs.**
   Wǒ méi yǒu zōngjiào xìnyǎng.
   (Wuh may yoh 'tz'-ong gee-ow shin yang.)

我没有宗教信仰。

3. I believe in ....
Wǒ xìn ... (Wuh shin ...) 我信 ...

* Catholicism   Tiānzhǔjiào (tee-an jew gee-ow) 天主教
* Christianity   Jīdūjiào (gee do gee-ow) 基督教
* Buddhism   Fójiào (foh-uh gee-ow) 佛教
* Taoism   Dàojiào (dow gee-ow) 道教
* Hinduism   Yìndùjiào (yin do gee-ow) 印度教
* Islam   Yīsīlánjiào ('e' si lan gee-ow) 伊斯兰教
* Judaism   Yóutàijiào (yoh tye gee-ow) 犹太教

TIPS

In China, people have the right and freedom to believe in any religion, and this is respected and protected by the central government. This is a sensitive topic with people around the world. It should only be discussed with those whom you are close to and those whom you are sure will be willing to openly discuss it with.

Accommodations
Zhùsù (Jew Sue) 住宿

1. I'd like to reserve a room.
   Wǒ xiǎng yùdìng yī ge fángjiān. (Wuh she-ang you ding 'e' guh fong gee-an.) 我想预定一个房间。

2. I've booked a room.
   Wǒ yǐjīng yùdìng le fángjiān. (Wuh 'e' jing you ding luh fong gee-an.) 我已经预定了房间。

3. I want to check in.
   Wǒ yào bànlǐ rùzhù.
   (Wuh yow ban lee roo jew.) 我要办理入住。

4. I don't know how long I will stay.
   Wǒ bù quèdìng yào dāi jǐ tiān. (Wuh boo chew-ay ding yow die gee tee-an.) 我不确定要待几天。

5. Do you have a ...?
   Nǐmen yǒu ... ma?
   (Knee men yoh ... ma?) 你们有 ... 吗?

* single room
  dānrénjiān (dan ren gee-an) 单人间
* double room
  shuāngrénjiān (shoe-ang ren gee-an) 双人间
* standard room
  biāozhǔnjiān (bee-ow jun gee-an) 标准间
* suite
  tàojiān (tow gee-an) 套间

---

6. He only stays at five star hotels.

Tā zhǐ zhù wǔxīngjíjiǔdiàn. (Ta jur jew woo shing gee-oh dee-an.) 他只住五星级酒店。

---

7. Do you have a vacant room for tomorrow?

Míngtiān shìfǒu yǒu kōng fángjiān?
(Ming tee-an sure foh yoh kong fong gee-an?)
明天是否有空房间？

---

8. How much will it cost?

Yào duōshao qián? (Yow doh-uh sh-ow chee-an?)
要多少钱？

---

9. Is there any discount?

Dǎzhé ma? (Da juh ma?) 打折吗？

---

10. Do I need to pay in advance?

Wǒ yào yùfù ma? (Wuh yow you foo ma?)
我要预付吗？

Let's
speak phrasebook
of mandarin
Chinese

11. Is a deposit required?

Yào jiāo yājīn ma? (Yow gee-ow yah gin ma?)

要交押金吗?

12. The room rate excludes taxes and the service charge.

Fáng fèi bù bāokuò shuì fèi hé fúwù fèi.

(Fong fay boo bao koh-uh 'sh'-way fay huh foo woo fay.) 房费不包括税费和服务费。

13. Does the room rate include breakfast?

Fáng fèi hán zǎocān ma?

(Fong fay han tzow 'ts'-an ma?) 房费含早餐吗?

14. Are hotel rooms more expensive in season?

Lǚyóu wàngjì shí fáng fèi huì hěn guì ma?

(Lü yoh wang gee sure fong fay hui hen 'g'way ma?)

旅游旺季时房费会很贵吗?

15. May I see the room?

Wǒ néng kànkan fángjiān ma?

(Wuh neng can can fong gee-an ma?)

我能看看房间吗?

16. We are full.

Méiyǒu fángjiān le.

(May yoh fong gee-an luh.) 没有房间了。

Amenities and Facilities
Fángjiān Shèshī (Fong Gee-an Shuh Sure)
房间设施

1. **I want a room on the south side.**
   Wǒ xiǎng yào yī ge yángmiàn de fángjiān.
   (Wuh she-ang yow 'e' guh yang me-an duh fong gee-an.) 我想要一个阳面的房间。

2. **Where's the elevator?**
   Diàntī zài nǎr? (Dee-an tee 'tz'-eye na?) 电梯在哪儿?

3. **Do you have hot water all day long?**
   Quántiān dōu gōngyìng rèshuǐ ma?
   (Chew-an Tee-an doe gong ying ruh 'sh'-way ma?)
   全天都供应热水吗?

4. **The toilet will not stop flushing.**
   Mǎtǒng de shuǐ liú ge bù tíng. (Ma tong duh 'sh'-way lee-oh guh boo ting.) 马桶的水流个不停。

5. **The ... doesn't work.**
   ... shì huài de. (... sure h-why duh.) ... 是坏的。

6. **Does the room have (a/n)...?**
   Fángjiān yǒu ... ma? (Fong gee-an yoh ... ma?)
   房间有 ... 吗?

Let's
speak
phrasebook
of mandarin
Chinese

* air-conditioner	kōngtiáo (kong tee-ow)	空调
* TV	diànshì (dee-an sure)	电视
* refrigerator	bīngxiāng (bing she-ang)	冰箱
* heating	nuǎnqì (new-an chee)	暖气
* remote control	yáokòngqì (yow kong chee)	遥控器
* electric outlet	diànyuán chāzuò (dee-an you-an chah 'z'-oh-uh)	电源插座
* safe	bǎoxiǎnxiāng (bao she-an she-ang)	保险箱
* toilet	wèishēngjiān (way sheng gee-an)	卫生间
* bathtub	yùgāng (you gang)	浴缸
* shower head	pēntóu (pen toe)	喷头
* bath towel	yùjīn (you gin)	浴巾
* shower cap	yù mào (you mao)	浴帽
* toilet soap	xiāngzào (she-ang tzow)	香皂
* toothbrush	yáshuā (yah shoe-ah)	牙刷
* toothpaste	yágāo (yah gow)	牙膏
* razor	tìxūdāo (tee shoe dow)	剃须刀
* toilet paper	wèishēngzhǐ (way sheng jur)	卫生纸
* garbage bin	lājī tǒng (la gee tong)	垃圾桶
* closestool	mǎtǒng (ma tong)	马桶
* ashtray	yānhuīgāng (yan hui gang)	烟灰缸
* pillow	zhěntou (jen toe)	枕头
* sheet	chuángdān (chew-ang dan)	床单
* quilt	bèizi (bay 'tz'-uh)	被子
* woolen blanket	máotǎn (mao tan)	毛毯
* slippers	tuōxié (toh-uh she-ay)	拖鞋
* electric kettle	diàn shuǐhú (dee-an 'sh'-way who)	电水壶

Hotel Service
Jiǔdiàn Fúwù (Gee-oh Dee-an Foo Woo)
酒店服务

1. **Do you have a?**

Nǐmen yǒu ... ma? (Knee men yoh ... ma?)
你们有 ... 吗？

* business center
  shāngwù zhōngxīn (shang woo zhong shin) 商务中心
* meeting room
  huìyìshì (hui 'e' sure) 会议室
* leisure center
  yúlè zhōngxīn (you luh zhong shin) 娱乐中心
* gymnasium
  jiànshēnfáng (gee-an shen fong) 健身房
* morning call service
  diànhuà jiào zǎo fúwù (dee-an hwa gee-ow tzow foo woo)
  电话叫早服务

2. **Will the porter carry my luggage to my room?**

Xíngli yuán huì bǎ wǒ de xíngli bān dào wǒ fángjiān
lǐ ma? (Shing lee you-an hui ba wuh duh shing lee
ban dow wuh fong gee-an ma?)
行李员会把我的行李搬到我房间里吗？

3. **My room number is ...**

Let's
speak
phrasebook
of mandarin
Chinese

Wǒ de fángjiān hào shì ...
(Wuh duh fong gee-an how sure ...) 我的房间号是 ...

---

4. **Do Not Disturb**

Qǐngwùdǎrǎo. (Ching woo da row.) 请勿打扰。

---

5. **Are there any messages for me?**

Yǒu rén gěi wǒ liúyán ma? (Yoh ren gay wuh lee-oh yan ma?) 有人给我留言吗？

---

6. **I can't lock my door.**

Wǒ suǒ bù shang fángmén le. (Wuh sew-uh boo shang fong men luh.) 我锁不上房门了。

---

7. **I left my room card in the room.**

Wǒ bǎ fáng kǎ là zài fángjiān lǐ le.
(Wuh ba fong ka la 'tz'-eye fong gee-an lee luh.)
我把房卡落在房间里了。

---

8. **Please bring breakfast to my room.**

Qǐng bǎ zǎocān sòng dào wǒ de fángjiān lǐ lái.
(Ching ba tzow 'ts'-an song dow wuh duh fong gee-an lee lie.) 请把早餐送到我的房间里来。

---

9. **Please clean my room.**

Qǐng bǎ wǒ de fángjiān dǎsǎo yī xià.
(Ching ba wuh duh fong gee-an da sow 'e' she-ah.)
请把我的房间打扫一下。

10. I'd like a 6 o'clock wake-up call tomorrow, please.

Qǐng zài míngtiān zǎoshang liù diǎn zhōng diànhuà jiào xǐng wǒ. (Ching 'tz'-eye ming tee-an tzow shang lee-oh dee-an zhong dee-an hwa gee-ow shing wuh.) 请在明天早上6点钟电话叫醒我。

---

11. Please iron this suit for me.

Qǐng bāng wǒ yùn yī xià zhè tào yīfu. (Ching bang wuh yun 'e' she-ah juh tow 'e' foo.) 请帮我熨一下这套衣服。

---

12. Has the laundry come back yet?

Xǐ de yīfu sòng huíláile ma? (She duh 'e' foo song hui lie luh ma?) 洗的衣服送回来了吗？

---

13. Can I make an international call?

Wǒ néng dǎ guójì chángtú ma? (Wuh neng da go-uh gee chang too ma?) 我能打国际长途吗？

Check-out
Jiézhàng (Gee-ay 'j'-ang) 结账

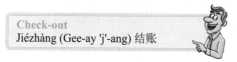

1. I want to check out.

Wǒ yào tuì fáng.
(Wuh yow too-ay fong.) 我要退房。

2. Could you please give back my deposit?

Let's
speak
phrasebook
of mandarin
Chinese

Qǐng wèn nǐ néng tuìhuán wǒ de yājīn ma? (Ching when, knee neng too-ay huan wuh duh yah gin ma?) 请问，你能退还我的押金吗？

---

3. **Please show me the bill.**

Qǐng gěi wǒ kàn yī xià zhàngdān. (Ching gay wuh can 'e' she-ah 'j'-ang dan.) 请给我看一下账单。

---

4. **Can I pay by credit card?**

Wǒ kěyǐ yòng xìnyòngkǎ jiézhàng ma? (Wuh kuh 'e' yong shin yong ka gee-ay 'j'-ang ma?) 我可以用信用卡结账吗？

---

5. **I've had a very enjoyable stay.**

Wǒ zài zhèr zhù de hěn yúkuài. (Wuh 'tz'-eye juh jew duh hen you kwai.) 我在这儿住得很愉快。

Renting a House
Zū Fáng (Tzoo Fong) 租房

1. **Where can I find (a/n)...?**

Nǎr yǒu ...? (Na yoh ...?) 哪儿有...？

* property company
 fángdìchǎn gōngsī (fong dee chan gong si) 房地产公司
* property management company

wùyè gōngsī (woo yeh gong si) 物业公司
* intermediary agent for house property
  zhōngjiè gōngsī (zhong gee-ay gong si) 中介公司

2. I'm looking for (a/n)...

Wǒ zài zhǎo yī ge ...
(Wuh 'tz'-eye 'j'-ow 'e' guh ...) 我在找一个 ...

* apartment
  gōngyù (gong you) 公寓
* villa
  biéshù (bee-eh shoe) 别墅
* mid-level storied building
  pǔtōng lóufáng (poo tong low fong) 普通楼房
* studio flat
  yījūshì gōngyù ('e' jew sure gong you)
  一居室公寓
* a place with two bedrooms and one living room
  liǎngshìyìtīng de fángzi
  (lee-ang sure 'e' ting duh fong 'tz'-uh) 两室一厅的房子
* one-bedroom place
  dānjūshì zhùfáng (dan jew sure jew fong)
  单居室住房
* fully-furnished apartment
  jiājù qíquán de fángzi
  (gee-ah jew chee chew-an duh fong 'tz'-uh) 家具齐全的房子

3. How many square meters?

Let's
speak
phrasebook
of mandarin
Chinese

Yǒu duōshao píngmǐ? (Yoh doh-uh sh-ow ping me?)

有多少平米？

4. How much is the rent?

Zūjīn duōshao? (Tzoo gin doh-uh sh-ow?)

租金多少？

5. Is there any (a/n) ... near by?

Fùjìn yǒu ... ma? (Foo gin yoh ... ma?)

附近有 ... 吗？

* laundry
  xǐyīfáng (she 'e' fong) 洗衣房
* phone bar
  huàbā (hwa ba) 话吧
* newsstand
  bàotíng (bao ting) 报亭
* grocery store
  záhuòdiàn (zah huo dee-an) 杂货店

6. When can I move in?

Wǒ shénme shíhòu néng bān jìnlái?

(Wuh shen muh sure hoh neng ban gin lie?)

我什么时候能搬进来？

7. Which floor?

Nǎ yī lóucéng? (Na 'e' low 'ts'-eng?) 哪一楼层？

8. This place is a dump.
Zhège dìfang tài pò le. (Juh guh dee fong tye poh-uh luh.) 这个地方太破了。

9. Who pays the ...?
Shuí fù ...? ('sh'-way foo ...?) 谁付 ...?

* management fee
  wùyè fèi (woo yeh fay) 物业费
* water bill
  shuǐ fèi ('sh'-way fay) 水费
* electricity bill
  diàn fèi (dee-an fay) 电费
* gas bill
  méiqì fèi (may chee fay) 煤气费
* telephone bill
  diànhuà fèi (dee-an hwa fay) 电话费
* heating fee
  nuǎnqì fèi (new-an chee fay) 暖气费
* cable TV bill
  yǒuxiàn diànshì fèi (yoh she-an dee-an sure fay) 有线电视费

10. Where can I pay the ...?
Zài nǎr néng jiāo ...? ('tz'-eye na neng gee-ow ...?) 在哪儿能交 ...?

11. What furniture is there?

Yǒu shénme jiājù? (Yoh shen muh gee-ah jew?)
有什么家具？

* bed
  chuáng (chew-ang) 床
* sofa
  shāfā (sha fah) 沙发
* wardrobe
  yīguì ('e''g'way) 衣柜
* closet
  bìchú (bee chew) 壁橱
* air conditioner
  kōngtiáo (kong tee-ow) 空调
* rug
  dìtǎn (dee tan) 地毯
* dinner table
  cānzhuō ('ts'-an joe-uh) 餐桌
* chair
  yǐzi ('e' 'tz'-uh) 椅子
* refrigerator
  bīngxiāng (bing she-ang) 冰箱
* stove
  zàojù (tzow jew) 灶具
* washing machine
  xǐyījī (she 'e' gee) 洗衣机
* water-heater
  rèshuǐqì (roo 'sh'-way chee) 热水器
* wash room
  wèishēngjiān (way sheng gee-an) 卫生间

* water cooler
  yǐnshuǐjī (yin 'sh'-way gee) 饮水机
* balcony
  yángtái (yang tye) 阳台
* cable TV
  yǒuxiàn diànshì (yoh sh-an dee-an sure) 有线电视
* double bed
  shuāngrénchuáng (shoe-ang ren chew-ang) 双人床
* single bed
  dānrénchuáng (dan ren chew-an) 单人床

12. **Everything is included.**

   Yīqiè dōu bāokuò le.

   ('e' chee-ay doe bao koh-uh luh.) 一切都包括了。

13. **The payment method is ...**

   Fù kuǎn fāngshì shì ...

   (Foo kuan fong sue sure ...) 付款方式是 ...

* monthly
  yuè fù (youeh-eh foo) 月付
* quarterly
  jì fù (gee foo) 季付
* half yearly
  bàn nián fù (ban knee-an foo) 半年付
* yearly
  nián fù (knee-an foo) 年付

Going out
Chūxíng (Chew Shing) 出行

Vehicles Jiāotōng Gōngjù
(Gee-ow Tong Gong Jew) 交通工具

* bus   gōnggòngqìchē (gong gong chee chuh) 公共汽车
* train   huǒchē (huo chuh) 火车
* ship / passenger liner   kèlún (kuh lun) 客轮
* airplane   fēijī (fay gee) 飞机
* taxi   chūzūchē (chew tzoo chuh) 出租车
* subway   dìtiě (dee tee-eh) 地铁
* bicycle   zìxíngchē ('tz'-uh shing chuh) 自行车
* motorcycle   mótuōchē (moh-uh toh-uh chuh) 摩托车

Direction & Orientation Fāngxiàng hé Fāngwèi
(Fong She-ang Huh Fong Way) 方向和方位

* east dōng (dong) 东	* left zuǒ ('z'-oh-uh) 左
* west xī (she) 西	* right yòu (yoh) 右
* south nán (nan) 南	* nearby fùjìn (foo gin) 附近
* north běi (bay) 北	* here zhèr (juh) 这儿
* front qián (chee-an) 前	* there nàr (na) 那儿
* back hòu (hou) 后	* where nǎr (na) 哪儿

* go straight ahead   yī zhí zǒu ('e' jur tzoh) 一直走
* turn around   diàotóu (dee-ow toe) 掉头

* opposite	duìmiàn ('d'-way me-an)	对面
* beside	pángbiān (pang bee-an)	旁边

* on	shàng (shang)	上
* above	shàngmiàn (shang me-an)	上面
* ahead	qiántou (chee-an toe)	前头
* inside	lǐmiàn (lee me-an)	里面
* enter	jìnrù (gin roo)	进入
* entry	rùkǒu (roo koh)	入口

* under	xià (she-ah)	下
* below	xiàmiàn (she-ah me-an)	下面
* behind	hòutou (hou toe)	后头
* outside	wàimiàn (why me-an)	外面
* exit	chūqù (chew chew)	出去
* exit	chūkǒu (chew koh)	出口

Asking for Directions
Wèn Lù (When Lu) 问路

1. **Excuse me, is there a ... near by?**
   Dǎrǎo le, qǐng wèn fùjìn yǒu ... ma?
   (Da row luh, ching when foo gin yoh ... ma?)
   打扰了，请问附近有 ... 吗？

2. **Can you tell me the way to ... please?**
   Can you direct me to ...?

外国人学说中国话

Qǐng wèn qù ... zěnme zǒu? (Ching when chew ...'tz'-en muh tzoh?) 请问去 ... 怎么走？

* Wangfujing Street
  Wángfǔjǐngdàjiē (wang foo jing da gee-ay) 王府井大街
* Xidan
  Xīdān (she dan) 西单
* Xiushui St
  Xiùshuǐjiē (she-oh 'sh'-way gee-ay) 秀水街
* Dazhalan
  Dàzhàlán (da zhah lan) 大栅栏
* Liulichang
  Liúlíchǎng (lee-oh lee chang) 琉璃厂
* Maliandao
  Mǎliándào (ma lee-an dow) 马连道

3. How far is it?
Dàgài yǒu duō yuǎn?
(Da guy yoh doh-uh you-an?) 大概有多远？

4. I want to go to…
Wǒ xiǎng qù ... (Wuh she-ang chew ...) 我想去 ...

* Beijing Hotel
  Běijīng Fàndiàn (bay jing fan dee-an) 北京饭店
* Novotel Xinqiao Hotel
  Xīnqiáo Fàndiàn (shin chee-ow fan dee-an) 新侨饭店

* Holiday Inn Downtown Beijing
  Běijīng Jīndūjiàrì Fàndiàn
  bay jing gin do chee-ah ree fan dee-an) 北京金都假日饭店
* Oriental Garden Hotel
  Dōngfānghuāyuán Fàndiàn
  (dong fong hwa you-an fan dee-an) 东方花园饭店
* Beijing Grand View Garden Hotel
  Běijīng Dàguānyuán Jiǔdiàn
  (bay jing da gu-on you-an gee-oh dee-an) 北京大观园酒店
* Jianguo Hotel Beijing
  Běijīng Jiànguó Fàndiàn
  (bay jing chee-an go-uh fan dee-an) 北京建国饭店
* Holiday Inn Lido Beijing
  Běijīng Lìdūjiàrì Fàndiàn
  (bay jing lee do chee-ah ree fan dee-an) 北京丽都假日饭店

5. How long will it take me to get there?
Dào nàr yào duō cháng shíjiān?
(Dow na yow doh-uh chang sure chee-an?)
到那儿要多长时间?

6. Can you show me the nearest way to the …?
Qǐng gàosù wǒ zuì jìn de … zěnme qù, hǎo ma?
(Ching gao sue wuh 'tz'-way gin duh … 'tz'-en muh chew, how ma?)
请告诉我最近的 … 怎么去, 好吗?

外国人学说中国话

* bus stop
gōnggòngqìchēzhàn (gong gong chee chuh jan)
公共汽车站
* shuttle bus
jīchǎng dàbā (gee chang da ba) 机场大巴
* railway station
huǒchēzhàn (huo chuh jan) 火车站
* subway stop
dìtiězhàn (dee tee-eh jan) 地铁站
* parking lot
tíngchēchǎng (ting chuh chang) 停车场
* restaurant
cāntīng ('ts'-an ting) 餐厅
* post office
yóujú (yoh jew) 邮局

7. **We got lost.**
Wǒmen mílù le. (Wuh men me lu luh.)
我们迷路了。

8. **Where am I?**
Wǒ zhè shì zài nǎr? (Wuh juh sure 'ts'-eye na?)
我这是在哪儿?

9. **Can I go to this place by …?**
Qù zhège dìfang néng chéng ... ma?
(Chew juh guh dee fong neng chung ... ma?)

去这个地方能乘 ... 吗？

---

10. **Go straight for about two minute.**
   Yīzhí wǎng qián zǒu dàyuē liǎng fēnzhōng.
   ('e' jur wang chee-an tzoh da you-eh lee-ang fen zhong.) 一直往前走大约两分钟。

---

11. **Turn left at the intersection.**
   Zài shízìlùkǒu xiàng zuǒ guǎi.
   ('tz'-eye sure 'tz'- uh lu koh she-ang 'z'-oh-uh gueye.) 在十字路口向左拐。

---

12. **Sorry, could you please say it again?**
   Duibuqǐ, qǐng nǐ zài jiǎng yī biàn, hǎo ma? ('d'-way boo chee, ching knee 'tz'-eye gee-ang 'e' bee-an, how ma?) 对不起，请你再讲一遍，好吗？

---

13. **Please mark it on my map for me.**
   Qǐng bāng wǒ biāo chūlái.
   (Ching bang wuh bee-ow chew lie.)
   请帮我标出来。

---

14. **How can I get to the place where the Olympic Games are being held?**
   Qù àoyùnhuì de ... bǐsài chǎngguǎn zěnme zǒu ne?
   (Chew ow yun hui duh ... bee sigh chang gu-on 'tz'- en muh tzoh nuh?)
   去奥运会的 ... 比赛场馆怎么走呢？

外国人学说中国话

Let's
speak
phrasebook
of mandarin
Chinese

PART 4

* National Aquatics Center
  Guójiā Yóuyǒng Zhōngxīn
  (go-uh gee-ah yoh yong zhong shin) 国家游泳中心
* National Indoor Stadium
  Guójiā Tǐyùguǎn (go-uh gee-ah tee you gu-on) 国家体育馆
* Beijing Shooting Range Hall
  Běijīng Shèjī Guǎn (bay jing shuh gee gu-on) 北京射击馆
* Wukesong Basketball Field
  Wǔkēsōng Lánqiú Guǎn (woo kuh song lan chee-oh gu-on)
  五棵松篮球馆
* Laoshan Velodrome
  Lǎoshān Zìxíngchē Guǎn
  (low shan 'tz'-uh shing chuh gu-on) 老山自行车馆
* China Agricultural University Gymnasium
  Zhōngguó Nóngyè Dàxué Tǐyùguǎn
  (zhong go-uh nong yeh da shoe-ay tee you gu-on)
  中国农业大学体育馆
* Peking University Gymnasium
  Běijīng Dàxué Tǐyùguǎn
  (bay jing da shoe-ay tee you gu-on) 北京大学体育馆
* Beijing Science and Technology University Gymnasium
  Běijīng Kējì Dàxué Tǐyùguǎn
  (bay jing kuh gee da shoe-ay tee you gu-on)
  北京科技大学体育馆
* Beijing University of Technology Gymnasium
  Běijīng Gōngyè Dàxué Tǐyùguǎn
  (bay jing gong yeh da shoe-ay tee you gu-on)
  北京工业大学体育馆

* Beijing Olympic Green Tennis Court
Àolínpǐkègōngyuán Wǎngqiú Zhōngxīn
(ow lin pee kuh gong you-an wang chee-oh zhong shin)
奥林匹克公园网球中心
* National Olympic Sports Center Gymnasium
Àotǐzhōngxīn Tǐyùguǎn
(ow tee zhong shin tee you gu-on) 奥体中心体育馆
* Beijing Workers' Stadium
Gōngrén Tǐyùchǎng (gong ren tee you chang)
工人体育场
* Beijing Workers' Gymnasium
Gōngrén Tǐyùguǎn (gong ren tee you gu-on)
工人体育馆
* Capital Gymnasium
Shǒudū Tǐyùguǎn (show do tee you gu-on) 首都体育馆
* Fengtai Sports Center Softball Field
Fēngtái Lěiqiú Chǎng (feng tye lay chee-oh chang)
丰台垒球场
* Yingdong Natatorium
Yīngdōng Yóuyǒng Guǎn (ying dong yoh yong gu-on)
英东游泳馆
* Beijing Institute of Technology Gymnasium
Běijīng Lǐgōng Dàxué Tǐyùguǎn
(bay jing lee gong da shoe-ay tee you gu-on)
北京理工大学体育馆
* Beijing Wukesong Sports Center Baseball Field
Wǔkēsōng Bàngqiú Chǎng
(woo kuh song bang chee-oh chang) 五棵松棒球场

外国人说中国话

Let's
speak
phrasebook
of mandarin
Chinese

PART 4

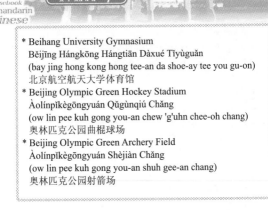

* Beihang University Gymnasium
  Běijīng Hángkōng Hángtiān Dàxué Tǐyùguǎn
  (bay jing hong kong hong tee-an da shoe-ay tee you gu-on)
  北京航空航天大学体育馆
* Beijing Olympic Green Hockey Stadium
  Àolínpǐkègōngyuán Qǔgùnqiú Chǎng
  (ow lin pee kuh gong you-an chew 'g'uhn chee-oh chang)
  奥林匹克公园曲棍球场
* Beijing Olympic Green Archery Field
  Àolínpǐkègōngyuán Shèjiàn Chǎng
  (ow lin pee kuh gong you-an shuh gee-an chang)
  奥林匹克公园射箭场

Buying Tickets
Mǎi Piào (My Pee-ow) 买票

1. Where can I buy a ticket?
   Zài nǎr mǎi piào? ('tz'-eye na my pee-ow?)
   在哪儿买票？

2. What's the difference between these two kinds of tickets?
   Zhè liǎng zhǒng piào yǒu shénme bù tóng?
   (Juh lee-ang zhog pee-ow yoh shen muh boo tong?)
   这两种票有什么不同？

3. **I'd like to book an air ticket to Shanghai.**
Wǒ dìng yī zhāng qù Shànghǎi de jīpiào.
(Wuh ding 'e' 'j'-ang chew shang hi duh gee pee-ow.)
我订一张去上海的机票。

4. **I'd like to reserve a soft berth ticket to Lhasa.**
Wǒ yào yùdìng qù Lāsà de wò pù.
(Wuh yow you ding chew la sah duh wuh poo.)
我要预订去拉萨的卧铺。

5. **How much is one ticket?**
Duōshao qián yī zhāng piào?
(Doh-uh sh-ow chee- an 'e' 'j'-ang pee-ow?)
多少钱一张票？

I would like to change my ticket, could you help me?
Wǒ xiǎng huàn piào, nǐ néng bāngzhù wǒ ma?

6. Can you give me a discount?
Néng bu néng dǎzhé?
(Neng boo neng da juh?) 能不能打折?

7. I would like to change my ticket, could you help me?
Wǒ xiǎng huàn piào, nǐ néng bāngzhù wǒ ma?
(Wuh she-ang huan pee-ow, knee neng bang jew wuh ma?) 我想换票，你能帮助我吗?

8. I want to change to a later flight.
Wǒ xiǎng huàn wǎn yīdiǎnr de hángbān.
(Wuh she-ang huan wan 'e' dee-an duh hong ban.)
我想换晚一点儿的航班。

9. I've lost my ticket.
Wǒ de piào diū le. (Wuh duh pee-ow dee-oh luh.)
我的票丢了。

10. I missed my train.
Wǒ méi gǎn shàng huǒchē.
(Wuh may gan shang huo chuh.) 我没赶上火车。

---

* buy a ticket
  mǎi piào (my pee-ow) 买票
* change a ticket
  huàn piào (huan pee-ow) 换票
* refund
  tuìpiào (too-ay pee-ow) 退票

* upgrade
  bǔpiào (boo pee-ow) 补票
* half-price ticket (esp for a child)
  bànpiào (ban pee-ow) 半票
* soft seat
  ruǎn zuò (roo-an 'z'-oh-uh) 软座
* hard seat
  yìng zuò (ying 'z'-oh-uh) 硬座
* upper berth
  shàng pù (shang poo) 上铺
* middle berth
  zhōng pù (zhong poo) 中铺
* lower berth
  xià pù (she-ah poo) 下铺
* airplane ticket
  fēijī piào (fay gee pee-ow) 飞机票
* first class
  tóuděng cāng (toe deng 'ts'-ang) 头等舱
* business class
  shāngwù cāng (shang woo 'ts'-ang) 商务舱
* economy class
  jīngjì cāng (jing gee 'ts'-ang) 经济舱
* single ticket
  dānchéng piào (dan chung pee-ow) 单程票
* round-trip ticket
  wǎngfǎn piào (wang fan pee-ow) 往返票
* train ticket
  huǒchē piào (huo chuh pee-ow) 火车票
* soft berth
  ruǎnwò (roo-an wuh) 软卧

外国人说中国话

let's
speak
phrasebook
of mandarin
Chinese

* hard berth
  yìngwò (ying wuh) 硬卧
* bus ticket
  gōngjiāo chēpiào (gong gee-ow chuh pee-ow) 公交车票
* bus station
  gōngjiāo chēzhàn (gong gee-ow chuh jan) 公交车站

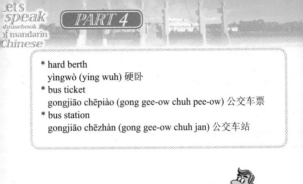

Luggage Xíngli (Shing Lee) 行李

1. Where is the …?

... zài nǎlǐ? (...'tz'-eye na lee?) ... 在哪里？

* lost luggage office
  Xíngli yíshī shēnbào chù
  (shing lee 'e' sure shen bow chew) 行李遗失申报处
* left-luggage office
  Xíngli jìcúnchù (shing lee gee 'ts'-un chew) 行李寄存处

2. Will you get the luggage labeled for Shanghai?
Qǐng bǎ wǒ de xíngli tuōyùn dào Shànghǎi, hǎo ma?
(Ching ba wuh duh shing lee toh-uh yun dow shang
hi, how ma?)
请把我的行李托运到上海好吗？

3. My luggage was lost.

wǒ méi zhǎo dào wǒ de xíngli. (wuh may 'j'-ow dow wuh duh shing lee.) 我没找到我的行李。

4. Can I check this bag too?

Néng bu néng bǎ zhège bāo yě zuò xíngli tuōyùn? (Neng boo neng ba juh guh bow yeh 'z'-oh-uh shing lee toh-uh yun?) 能不能把这个包也作行李托运？

5. Where can I get my luggage?

Dào nǎlǐ qù qǔ wǒ de xíngli? (Dow na lee chew chew wuh duh shing lee?) 到哪里去取我的行李？

6. My luggage is damaged.

Wǒ de xíngli bèi sǔnhuài le. (Wuh duh shing lee bay sun h-why luh.) 我的行李被损坏了。

7. Where can I get a luggage cart?

Wǒ zài nǎlǐ kěyǐ zhǎo dào xíngli tuī chē? (Wuh 'ts'-eye na lee kuh 'e' 'j'-ow dow shing lee too-ay chuh?) 我在哪里可以找到行李推车？

Taking an Airplane
Chéng Fēijī (Chung Fay Gee) 乘飞机

外国人学说中国话

1. I'd like to have a seat by the window.

Wǒ yào yī ge kào chuāng de zuòwèi.

(Wuh yow 'e' guh cow chew-ang duh 'z'-oh-uh way.)

我要一个靠窗的座位。

---

2. **I will fly to ... tomorrow. The flight number is ...**

Wǒ míngtiān qù ... Hángbān hào shì ...

(Wuh ming tee-an chew ... Hong ban how sure ...)

我明天去 ... 航班号是 ...

---

3. **I'd like to change my reservation.**

Wǒ xiǎng biàngēng yī xià wǒ de yùdìng.

(Wuh she-ang bee-an geng 'e' she-ah wuh duh you ding.) 我想变更一下我的预订。

---

4. **I'd like to reconfirm my flight from Beijing to ...**

Wǒ xiǎng quèrèn yī xià cóng běijīng dào ... de bānjī.

(Wuh she-ang chew-ay ren 'e' she-ah 'ts'-ong bay jing dow ... duh ban gee.)

我想确认一下从北京到 ... 的班机。

---

5. **The flight is fully booked.**

Zhè ge hángbān méi yǒu kòng wèi le. (Juh guh hong ban may yoh kong way luh.) 这个航班没有空位了。

---

6. **The flight is cancelled.**

Hángbān qǔxiāo le. (Hong ban chew she-ow luh.)

航班取消了。

7. Where should I check in for this flight?

Zhè tàng hángbān zài nǎr bànlǐ dēng jī shǒuxù? (J
tang hong ban 'tz'-eye na ban lee deng gee show
shoe?) 这趟航班在哪儿办理登机手续？

---

8. What is the boarding time?

Hé shí dēng jī? (Huh sure deng gee?) 何时登机？

---

9. What time does it take off / arrive?

Jǐ diǎn qǐfēi / dào? (Gee dee-an chee fay / dow?)
几点起飞／到？

---

10. How long will the flight be delayed?

Bānjī yánwù duō cháng shíjiān? (Ban gee yan woo
doh-uh chang sure gee-an?) 班机延误多长时间？

---

11. Where is my seat?

Wǒ de zuòwèi zài nǎlǐ? (Wuh duh 'z'-oh-uh way 'tz'-
eye na lee?) 我的座位在哪里？

---

12. What kind of drinks do you have?

Fēijī shàng tígòng nǎxiē yǐnliào?
(Fay gee shang tee gong na she-ay yin lee-ow?)
飞机上提供哪些饮料？

---

13. Can I put my baggage here?

Wǒ néng jiāng shǒu tí xíngli fàng zài zhèr ma?
(Wuh neng gee-ang show tee shing lee fong 'tz'-eye

外国人学说中国话

能将手提行李放在这儿吗？

'j'-ow) 护照

* visa
  qiānzhèng (chee-an jung) 签证
* things to declare
  shēnbào (shen bow) 申报
* nothing to declare
  wú shēnbào (woo shen bow) 无申报
* green channel
  lǜsè tōngdào (lü suh tong dow) 绿色通道
* duty-free items
  miǎn shuì shāngpǐn (me-an 'sh'-way shang pin)
  免税商品
* currency declaration
  huòbì shēnbào (huo bee shen bow) 货币申报
* international flight
  guójì hángbān (go-uh gee hong ban) 国际航班
* domestic flight
  guónèi hángbān (go-uh nay hong ban) 国内航班
* boarding
  dēng jī kǒu (deng gee koh) 登机口
* flight number
  hángbān hào (hong ban how) 航班号

我想改签
硬卧 可以吗？

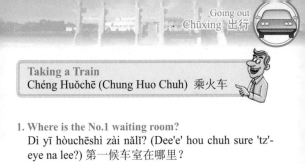

Taking a Train
Chéng Huǒchē (Chung Huo Chuh) 乘火车

1. **Where is the No.1 waiting room?**
   Dì yī hòuchēshì zài nǎlǐ? (Dee'e' hou chuh sure 'tz'-eye na lee?) 第一候车室在哪里？

2. **Where do I get my ticket punched?**
   Wǒ zài nǎr jiǎnpiào?
   (Wuh 'tz'-eye na gee-an pee-ow?) 我在哪儿检票？

3. **What time are the trains to …?**
   Qù … de huǒchē dōu yǒu jǐ diǎn de?
   (Chew … duh huo chuh doe yoh gee dee-an duh?)
   去 … 的火车都有几点的？

4. **Which platform does the Tianjin train leave from?**
   Kāi wǎng Tiānjīn de huǒchē zài dì jǐ zhàntái shàng chē? ('k'-eye wang tee-an gin duh huo chuh 'tz'-eye dee gee jan tye shang chuh?)
   开往天津的火车在第几站台上车？

5. **Will the train arrive on time?**
   Huǒchē huì zhǔnshí dàodá ma? (Huo chuh hui jun sure dow da ma?) 火车会准时到达吗？

外国人学说中国话

* station hall
chēzhàn dàtīng (chuh jan da ting) 车站大厅
* information desk
fúwù tái (foo wooo tye) 服务台
* waiting room
hòuchēshì (hou chuh sure) 候车室
* enquiry office
wèn xùn chù (when sh-une chew) 问讯处
* platform-ticket
yàn piào kǒu (yan pee-ow koh) 验票口
* platform
zhàntái (jan tye) 站台
* express train
tèkuài (tuh kwai) 特快
* direct train
zhíkuài (jur kwai) 直快
* bullet train
pǔkuài (poo kwai) 普快
* way train
mànchē (man chuh) 慢车
* up train
shàngxíng chē (shang shing chuh) 上行车
* down train
xiàxíng chē (she-ah shing chuh) 下行车
* carriage, coach
chēxiāng (chuh she-ang) 车厢
* dining car
cānchē ('ts'-an chuh) 餐车
* smoking area
xīyān qū (she yan chew) 吸烟区

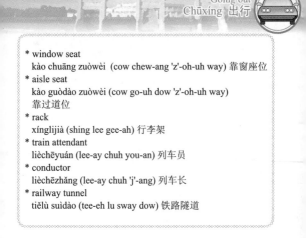

* window seat
  kào chuāng zuòwèi (cow chew-ang 'z'-oh-uh way) 靠窗座位
* aisle seat
  kào guòdào zuòwèi (cow go-uh dow 'z'-oh-uh way)
  靠过道位
* rack
  xínglijià (shing lee gee-ah) 行李架
* train attendant
  lièchēyuán (lee-ay chuh you-an) 列车员
* conductor
  lièchēzhǎng (lee-ay chuh 'j'-ang) 列车长
* railway tunnel
  tiělù suìdào (tee-eh lu sway dow) 铁路隧道

6. **The train was 10 minutes late.**
   Huǒchē wǎn diǎn le shí fēnzhōng.
   (Huo chuh wan dee-an luh sure fen zhong.)
   火车晚点了10分钟。

7. **What's the next stop?**
   Huǒchē xià yī zhàn shì nǎr?
   (Huo chuh she-ah 'e' jan sure na?)
   火车下一站是哪儿?

外国人学说中国话

Let's
speak
phrasebook
of mandarin
Chinese

PART 4

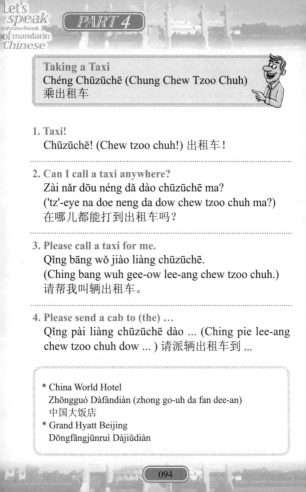

Taking a Taxi
Chéng Chūzūchē (Chung Chew Tzoo Chuh)
乘出租车

1. **Taxi!**
   Chūzūchē! (Chew tzoo chuh!) 出租车！

2. **Can I call a taxi anywhere?**
   Zài nǎr dōu néng dǎ dào chūzūchē ma?
   ('tz'-eye na doe neng da dow chew tzoo chuh ma?)
   在哪儿都能打到出租车吗？

3. **Please call a taxi for me.**
   Qǐng bāng wǒ jiào liàng chūzūchē.
   (Ching bang wuh gee-ow lee-ang chew tzoo chuh.)
   请帮我叫辆出租车。

4. **Please send a cab to (the) ...**
   Qǐng pài liàng chūzūchē dào ... (Ching pie lee-ang chew tzoo chuh dow ...) 请派辆出租车到 ...

---

* China World Hotel
  Zhōngguó Dàfàndiàn (zhong go-uh da fan dee-an)
  中国大饭店
* Grand Hyatt Beijing
  Dōngfāngjūnruì Dàjiǔdiàn

(dong fong jun roo-'e' da gee-oh dee-an) 东方君悦大酒店

* The Peninsula Palace Beijing
  Běijīng Wángfǔ Fàndiàn (bay jing wang foo fan dee-an)
  北京王府饭店

* Presidential Plaza Beijing
  Guóbīn Jiǔdiàn (go-uh bin gee-oh dee-an) 国宾酒店

* Hilton Beijing
  Běijīng Xīěrdùn Jiǔdiàn
  (bay jing she are dun gee-oh dee-an) 北京希尔顿酒店

* The St. Regis Beijing
  Guójì Jùlèbù Fàndiàn (go-uh gee jew luh boo fan dee-an)
  国际俱乐部饭店

* Beijing Kunlun Hotel
  Běijīng Kūnlún Fàndiàn (bay jing 'k'uhn lun fan dee-an)
  北京昆仑饭店

* Shangri-La Hotel Beijing
  Běijīng Xiānggélǐlā Fàndiàn
  (bay jing she-ang guh lee la fan dee-an) 北京香格里拉饭店

* Diaoyutai State Guesthouse
  Diàoyútái Guóbīnguǎn (dee-ow you tye go-uh bin gu-on)
  钓鱼台国宾馆

5. **Are you working right now?**
   Nǐ zǒu ma? (Knee tzoh ma?) 你走吗?

6. **Please take me to (the)…**
   Qǐng sòng wǒ qù … (Ching song wuh chew …)
   请送我去…

7. Drop me at (the)…

Wǒ zài ... xià chē. (Wuh 'tz'-eye ... she-ah chuh.)

我在...下车。

* Tian'anmen Square
  Tiānanmén Guǎngchǎng (tee-an an men 'g'wang chang)
  天安门广场
* Summer Palace
  Yíhéyuán ('e' huh you-an) 颐和园
* Forbidden City
  Gùgōng (goo gong) 故宫
* Zhongshan Park
  Zhōngshān Gōngyuán (zhong shan gong you-an)
  中山公园
* Fragrant Hill Park
  Xiāngshān Gōngyuán (she-ang shan gong you-an)
  香山公园
* Beihai (North Sea) Park
  Běihǎi Gōngyuán (bay hi gong you-an) 北海公园
* China's Science and Technology Museum
  Zhōngguó Kēxuéjìshù Guǎn
  (zhon go-uh kuh shoe-ay gee shoe gu-on) 中国科学技术馆
* Joyful Pavilion (Tao Ran Ting) Park
  Táorántíng Gōngyuán (tow ran ting gong you-an)
  陶然亭公园
* Beijing Amusement Park
  Běijīng Yóulèyuán (bay jing yoh luh you-an)
  北京游乐园
* Temple of Heaven
  Tiāntán Gōngyuán (tee-an tan gong you-an) 天坛公园

8. I want to go to this place. Here is the address.

Wǒ yào qù zhège dìfang. Zhè shì dìzhǐ.

(Wuh yow chew juh guh dee fong. Juh sure dee jur.)

我要去这个地方。这是地址。

---

9. Can we get there within 20 minutes?

Èrshí fēnzhōng néng dào nàr ma?

(Are sure fen zhong neng dow na ma?)

20分钟能到那儿吗?

---

10. I'd like to look around the city, if you don't mind.

Rúguǒ nǐ bù jièyì, wǒ xiǎng kànkan jiē jǐng.

(Roo go-uh knee boo gee-ay 'e', wuh she-ang can can gee-ay jing.)

如果你不介意, 我想看看街景。

---

11. Is this the right road?

Zhè tiáo lù duì ma? (Juh tee-ow lu 'd'-way ma?)

这条路对吗?

---

12. How much do I owe you?

Wǒ gāi fù duōshao qián?

(Wuh guy foo doh-uh sh-ow chee-an?)

我该付多少钱?

---

13. Stop here.

Tíng zhèr ba. (Ting juh ba.)

停这儿吧。

外国人学说

14. I'm getting out.

Wǒ zài zhèr xià chē.

(Wuh 'tz'-eye juh she-ah chuh.)

我在这儿下车。

---

15. Please open the trunk.

Qǐng dǎ kāi hòubèixiāng.

(Ching da 'k'-eye hou bay she-ang.)

请打开后备箱。

---

16. Do you have change?

Nǐ yǒu língqián ma?

(Knee yoh ling chee-an ma?)

你有零钱吗?

---

17. I don't have any change.

Wǒ méiyǒu língqián. (Wuh may yoh ling chee-an.)

我没有零钱。

---

18. Keep the change.

Bù yòng zhǎo le. (Boo yong 'j'-ow luh.)

不用找了。

---

19. Please give me a receipt.

Wǒ yào yī zhāng fāpiào.

(Wuh yow 'e' 'j'-ang fah pee-ow.)

我要一张发票。

* taximeter
jìjiàqì (gee gee-ah che) 计价器
* distance
jùlí (jew lee) 距离
* far
yuǎn (you-an) 远
* near
jìn (gin) 近
* seat belt
ānquándài (an chew-an die) 安全带
* slow down
màn diǎnr (man dee-an) 慢点儿
* hurry up
kuài diǎnr (kwai dee-an) 快点儿
* wait a minute
děng huìr (deng hui) 等会儿
* red light
hóngdēng (hong deng) 红灯
* green light
lǜdēng (lü deng) 绿灯
* traffic jam
dǔ chē (do chuh) 堵车
* side road
fǔlù (foo lu) 辅路
* highway
gāosùlù (gow suh lu) 高速路
* living area / compound
xiǎoqū (she-ow chew) 小区

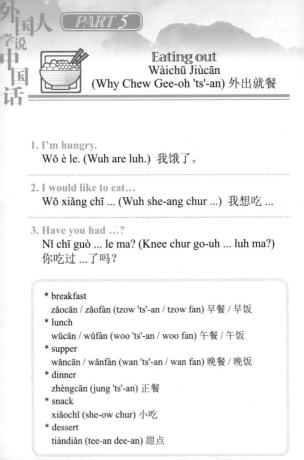

Eating out
Wàichū Jiùcān
(Why Chew Gee-oh 'ts'-an) 外出就餐

1. **I'm hungry.**
   Wǒ è le. (Wuh are luh.) 我饿了。

2. **I would like to eat…**
   Wǒ xiǎng chī ... (Wuh she-ang chur ...) 我想吃 ...

3. **Have you had …?**
   Nǐ chī guò ... le ma? (Knee chur go-uh ... luh ma?)
   你吃过 ... 了吗?

---

* breakfast
  zǎocān / zǎofàn (tzow 'ts'-an / tzow fan) 早餐 / 早饭
* lunch
  wǔcān / wǔfàn (woo 'ts'-an / woo fan) 午餐 / 午饭
* supper
  wǎncān / wǎnfàn (wan 'ts'-an / wan fan) 晚餐 / 晚饭
* dinner
  zhèngcān (jung 'ts'-an) 正餐
* snack
  xiǎochī (she-ow chur) 小吃
* dessert
  tiándiǎn (tee-an dee-an) 甜点

4. **Would you like to go to a …?**

Nǐ xiǎng qù ... ma?

(Knee she-ang chew ... ma?) 你想去 ... 吗?

---

* Chinese restaurant
  zhōngcān fànguǎnr (zhong 'ts'-an fan gu-on) 中餐饭馆儿
* Western restaurant
  xīcāntīng (she 'ts'-an ting) 西餐厅
* Japanese restaurant
  rìběnliàolǐ diàn (ree ben lee-ow lee dee-an) 日本料理店
* fast-food restaurant
  kuàicān diàn (kwai 'ts'-an dee-an) 快餐店
* vegetarian restaurant
  sùshí cāntīng (sue sure 'ts'-an ting) 素食餐厅

---

5. **Do you have any seats?**

Yǒu zuòwèi ma? (Yoh 'z'-oh-uh way ma?)
有座位吗?

---

6. **I would like to see the menu.**

Wǒ xiǎng kànkan càidān.
(Wuh she-ang can can 'ts'-eye dan.) 我想看看菜单。

---

7. **Do you have an English menu ?**

Yǒu yīngwén càidān ma?
(Yoh ying when 'ts'-eye dan ma?) 有英文菜单吗?

---

8. **Cheers!**

Let's
speak
phrasebook
of mandarin
Chinese

Gānbēi (Gan bay!) 干杯！

---

9. What's today's special?

Jīntiān de tèsè cài shì shénme? (Gin tee-an duh tuh suh 'ts'-eye sure shen muh?) 今天的特色菜是什么？

---

10. What kind of flavor does it have ?

Zhè dào cài shì shénme kǒuwèi de?
(Juh dow 'ts'-eye sure shen muh koh way duh?)
这道菜是什么口味的？

Flavor Kǒuwèi (Koh Way) 口味

* sour   suān (sue-an) 酸
* sweet   tián (tee-an) 甜
* bitter   kǔ (koo) 苦
* hot   là (la) 辣
* salty   xián (she-an) 咸

---

11. I can use chopsticks.

Wǒ huì yòng kuàizi.
(Wuh hui yong kwai 'tz'-uh.) 我会用筷子。

---

12. Is it good?

Hǎo chī ma? (How chur ma?) 好吃吗？

---

13. Are you full?

Nǐ chībǎole ma? (Knee chur bow luh ma?)

你吃饱了吗？

14. **Check, please.**

Fúwùyuán, jiézhàng.

(Foo woo you-an, gee-ay 'j'-ang.) 服务员，结账。

15. **Excuse me, please put the leftovers in a box.**

Fúwùyuán, dǎbāo. (Foo woo you-an, da bow.)
服务员，打包。

16. **Let's go Dutch.**

Zánmen gè fù gè de ba. ('tz'-an men guh foo guh
duh ba.) 咱们各付各的吧。

17. **Waiter / Waitress, we need another ...**

Fúwùyuán, qǐng zài gěi wǒmen ..., hǎo ma?
(Foo woo you-an, ching 'tz'-eye gay wuh men ...,
how ma?) 服务员，请再给我们 ...，好吗？

* coffee pot	kāfēi hú (ka fay who)	咖啡壶
* napkin	cānjīnzhǐ ('ts'-an gin jur)	餐巾纸
* tablecloth	zhuōbù (joe-uh boo)	桌布
* teapot	cháhú (chah who)	茶壶
* tea set	chájù (chah jew)	茶具
* dish	diézi (dee-eh 'tz'-uh)	碟子
* plate	pánzi (pan 'tz'-uh)	盘子
* bowl	wǎn (wan)	碗

Let's
speak
phrasebook
of mandarin
Chinese!

* soup spoon	tāngchí (tang chur)	汤匙
* knife	cāndāo ('ts'-an dow)	餐刀
* cup	bēizi (bay 'tz'-uh)	杯子
* glass	bōlibēi (boh-uh lee bay)	玻璃杯
* toothpick	yáqiān (yah chee-an)	牙签

Menu Càipǔ ('ts'-eye Poo) 菜谱

* stir-fried	chǎo de (chow duh)	炒的
* roasted	kǎo de (cow duh)	烤的
* boiled	zhǔ de (jew duh)	煮的
* fried	zhá de (zhah duh)	炸的
* steamed	zhēng de (jung duh)	蒸的
* raw	shēng de (sheng duh)	生的

Pork   Zhū Ròu (Jew Row) 猪肉

* stewed pork with brown sauce
  hóngshāo ròu (hong sh-ow row) 红烧肉
* stir-fried pork fillet in brown sauce
  jīng jiàng ròu sī (jing gee-ang row si) 京酱肉丝
* shredded pork with garlic sauce
  yú xiāng ròu sī (you she-ang row si) 鱼香肉丝
* stir-fried shredded pork with egg-white sauce
  fúróng ròu sī (foo rong row si) 芙蓉肉丝
* twice-cooked pork slices
  huí guō ròu (hui go-uh row) 回锅肉
* fried diced pork in soy sauce
  jiàng bào ròu dīng (gee-ang bow row ding) 酱爆肉丁
* sweet-and-sour pork with pineapple
  bōluó gū lǎo ròu (boh-uh low-uh goo low row) 菠萝咕咾肉
* steamed pork with preserved vegetables
  méi cài kòu ròu (may 'ts'-eye koh row) 梅菜扣肉
* omelet with shredded pork
  mù xū ròu (moo shoe row) 木须肉
* sauteed fillet with thick gravy
  huá liū lǐji (hwa lee-oh lee gee) 滑溜里脊
* sweet and sour pork fillet
  táng cù lǐji (tang 'ts'-oo lee gee) 糖醋里脊
* soft-fried fillet
  ruǎn zhà lǐji (roo-an zhah lee gee) 软炸里脊
* spareribs with brown sauce
  hóngshāo páigǔ (hong sh-ow pie goo) 红烧排骨

Let's
speak
phrasebook
of mandarin
Chinese

* sweet-and-sour spareribs
  táng cù páigǔ (tang 'ts'-oo pie goo) 糖醋排骨
* steamed spareribs with rice flower
  fěn zhēng páigǔ (fen jung pie goo) 粉蒸排骨
* stewed meatballs with brown sauce
  hóngshāo shīzitóu (hong sh-ow sure 'tz'-uh toe)
  红烧狮子头
* meatballs en casserole
  shāguō wánzi (sha go-uh wan 'tz'-uh) 砂锅丸子
* pork leg braised in brown sauce
  hóngshāo zhǒuzi (hong sh-ow joe 'tz'-uh) 红烧肘子
* pork joint stewed with crystal sugar
  bīngtáng zhǒuzi (bing tang joe 'tz'-uh) 冰糖肘子
* stewed sliced ham with white gourd
  dōngguā huǒtuǐ (dong guah huo too-ay) 冬瓜火腿
* roasted sucking pig
  kǎo rǔ zhū (cow roo jew) 烤乳猪
* shredded pork and haricot bean
  ròu sī biǎndòu (row si bee-an doe) 肉丝扁豆
* vermicelli with spicy minced pork
  mǎyǐ shàng shù (ma 'e' shang shoe) 蚂蚁上树
* stewed pig's trotters
  dùn zhū tí (dun jew tee) 炖猪蹄
* fried pig's liver
  chǎo zhū gān (cow jew gan) 炒猪肝
* quick-fried liver with distilled grains sauce
  liū gān jiān (lee-oh gan gee-an) 熘肝尖
* quick stir-fried pig's kidney
  huǒ bào yāohuā (huo bow yow hwa) 火爆腰花

* shredded tripe with chilli sauce
  hóng yóu dǔ sī (hong yoh do si) 红油肚丝
* boiled sliced pork
  bái qiē ròu (buy chee-ay row) 白切肉
* barbeque pork (Cantonese style)
  chāshāo ròu (chah sh-ow row) 叉烧肉

Beef   Niú Ròu (Knee-oh Row) 牛肉

* fried curried beef
  gālí niú ròu (ga lee knee-oh row) 咖喱牛肉
* beef with oyster sauce
  háoyóu niú ròu (how yoh knee-oh row) 蚝油牛肉
* beef boiled in hot chilli sauce
  shuǐ zhǔ niú ròu ('sh'-way jew knee-oh row) 水煮牛肉
* beef fillets roasted on the iron plate
  tiě bǎn niú ròu (tee-eh ban knee-oh row) 铁板牛肉
* spiced beef
  jiàng niú ròu (gee-ang knee-oh row) 酱牛肉
* braised beef tenderloin chunks with soy sauce
  hóngshāo niúnǎn (hong sh-ow knee-oh nan) 红烧牛腩
* braised beef with soy sauce
  hóng mèn niú ròu (hong men knee-oh row) 红焖牛肉
* stewed ox tail with brown sauce
  hóngshāo niú wěi (hong sh-ow knee-oh way) 红烧牛尾

Let's
speak
phrasebook
of mandarin
Chinese

* fried tripe
  bào niú dǔ (bow knee-oh do) 爆牛肚

Mutton　Yáng Ròu (Yang Row) 羊肉

* fried mutton slice with green scallion
  cōng bào yáng ròu ('ts'-ong bow yang row) 葱爆羊肉
* boiled mutton
  shǒu zhuā yáng ròu (show jew-ah yang row) 手抓羊肉
* cooked chopped lamb's offal
  yáng zá suì (yang zah sway) 羊杂碎
* braised mutton with soy sauce
  hóng mèn yáng ròu (hong men yang row) 红焖羊肉
* instant-boiled mutton Mongolian hot pot
  shuàn yáng ròu ('sh'-why yang row) 涮羊肉
* roasted mutton cubes on spit
  yáng ròu chuàn (yang row chew-an) 羊肉串

Chicken　Jī Ròu (Gee Row) 鸡肉

* sauteed chicken cubes with chilli and peanuts
  gōng bǎo jī dīng (gong bow gee ding) 宫保鸡丁
* quick-fried diced chicken in bean sauce

jiàng bào jī dīng (gee-ang bow gee ding) 酱爆鸡丁

* sliced chicken with mushroom

  mógu jī piàn (moh-uh goo gee pee-an) 蘑菇鸡片

* sauteed sliced chicken with bamboo shoots

  dōngsǔn jī piàn (dong sun gee pee-an) 冬笋鸡片

* beggar's chicken (baked chicken)

  jiào huà jī (gee-ow hwa gee) 叫化鸡

* yunnan-style steamed chicken

  qì guō jī (chee go-uh gee) 汽锅鸡

* grilled chicken

  shāo jī (sh-ow gee) 烧鸡

* savory and crisp chicken

  xiāng sū jī (she-ang suh gee) 香酥鸡

* General Zuǒ's chicken

  zuǒ zōng táng jī ('z'-oh-uh 'tz'-ong tang gee) 左宗棠鸡

Duck   Yā Ròu (Yah Row) 鸭肉

* roast Beijing duck

  Běijīng kǎo yā (bay jing cow yah) 北京烤鸭

* smoked duck

  zhāng chá yā ('j'-ang chah yah) 樟茶鸭

* steamed Nanjing duck

  Nánjīng bǎn yā (nan jing ban yah) 南京板鸭

Let's
speak
phrasebook
of mandarin
Chinese

Seafood　Hǎixiān (Hi She-an) 海鲜

* fish stewed in brown sauce
  hóngshāo yú (hong sh-ow you) 红烧鱼
* sweet and sour fish
  táng cù yú (tang 'ts'-oo you) 糖醋鱼
* steamed fish
  qīngzhēng yú (ching jung you) 清蒸鱼
* boil shrimp
  bái zhuó xiā (buy joe-uh she-ah) 白灼虾
* spicy salt shrimp
  jiāoyán xiā (gee-ow yan she-ah) 椒盐虾
* Sichuan style crab
  xiāng là xiè (she-ang la she-ay) 香辣蟹
* special style lobster
  shàng tāng jú lóng xiā (shang tang jew long she-ah)
  上汤焗龙虾
* steam live rock cod
  qīngzhēng shí bān yú (ching jung sure ban you)
  清蒸石斑鱼

Vegetarian　Sùcài (Suh 'ts'-eye) 素菜

* ried bean curd / tofu
  hóngshāo dòufu (hong sh-ow doe foo) 红烧豆腐

* stir-fried bean curd in spicy sauce
  má pó dòufu (ma poo doe foo) 麻婆豆腐
* tender greens with mushrooms
  xiānggū cài xīn (she-ang goo 'ts'eye shin) 香菇菜心
* lettuce stir-fried in oyster sauce
  háoyóu shēngcài (how yoh sheng 'ts'-eye) 蚝油生菜
* fried string beans
  gān biān sìjìdòu (gan bee-an si gee doe) 干煸四季豆
* fish-flavored shredded eggplant
  yú xiāng qiézi (you she-ang chee-ay 'tz'-uh) 鱼香茄子
* stewed eggplant with brown sauce
  shāo qiézi (sh-ow chee-ay 'tz'-uh) 烧茄子
* pine nuts with sweet corn
  sōngrén yùmǐ (song ren you me) 松仁玉米

Seasoning   Zuòliao ('z'-oh-uh Lee-ow) 作料

* ginger
  jiāng (gee-ang) 姜
* scallion / onion
  cōng / yángcōng ('ts'-ong / yang 'ts'-ong) 葱/洋葱
* parsley
  xiāngcài (she-ang 'ts'-eye) 香菜
* salt
  yán (yan) 盐

* MSG
  wèijīng (way jing) 味精
* black pepper
  hēi hújiāo fěn (hay hoo gee-ow fen) 黑胡椒粉
* cumin
  zīrán ('tz'-uh ran) 孜然
* soy sauce
  jiàngyóu (gee-ang yoh) 酱油
* vinegar
  cù ('ts'-oo) 醋
* chili sauce
  làjiāo jiàng (la gee-ow gee-ang) 辣椒酱
* ketchup
  fānqié jiàng (fan chee-ay gee-ang) 蕃茄酱
* mustard
  jièmo (gee-ay moh-uh) 芥末
* curry
  gālí (ga lee) 咖喱

Soup   Tāng (Tang) 汤

* laver and egg soup
  zǐcài dàn huā tāng ('tz'-uh 'ts'-eye dan hwa tang)
  紫菜蛋花汤
* hot and sour soup

suān là tāng (sue-an la tang) 酸辣汤

* fish ball soup
  yú wán tāng (you wan tang) 鱼丸汤
* pickled mustard tuber and pork soup
  zhàcài ròu sī tāng (zhah 'ts'-eye row si tang) 榨菜肉丝汤
* bean curd soup
  dòufu tāng (doe foo tang) 豆腐汤
* minced chicken and corn pottage
  jī róng sù mǐ tāng (gee rong sue me tang) 鸡茸粟米汤

Staple Food   Zhǔshí (Jew Sure) 主食

* plain white rice
  bái fàn (buy fan) 白饭
* egg fried rice
  dàn chǎo fàn (dan chow fan) 蛋炒饭
* fried rice of Yangzhou style
  Yángzhōu chǎo fàn (yang joe chow fan) 扬州炒饭
* rice porridge
  xī fàn / zhōu (she fan / joe) 稀饭 / 粥
* noodles
  miàntiáo (me-an tee-ow) 面条
* noodles with soup
  tāngmiàn (tang me-an) 汤面
* fried noodles

chǎomiàn (chow me-an) 炒面
* stretched noodles
lāmiàn (la me-an) 拉面
* beef noodles
niú ròu miàn (knee-oh row me-an) 牛肉面
* noodles with fried soybean paste
zhá jiàng miàn (zhah gee-ang me-an) 炸酱面
* sliced noodles
dāoxiāomiàn (dao she-ow me-an) 刀削面
* Sichuan style noodles with pepper sauce
dān dān miàn (dan dan me-an) 担担面
* sesame paste noodles
májiàng miàn (ma gee-ang me-an) 麻酱面
* rice noodles
mǐfěn (me fen) 米粉
* boiled dumplings
shuǐjiǎo ('sh'-way gee-ow) 水饺
* steamed dumplings
zhēngjiǎo (jung gee-ow) 蒸饺
* wontons
húntun (hun tun) 馄饨
* steamed buns
mántou (man toe) 馒头
* steamed twisted roll
huājuǎn (hwa jew-an) 花卷
* clay oven rolls
shāobing (sh-ow bing) 烧饼
* fried bread stick
yóutiáo (yoh tee-ow) 油条

* cruller
  yóubǐng (yoh bing) 油饼
* steamed bread with stuffings
  bāozi (bow 'tz'-uh) 包子
* fried dumplings
  guōtiēr (go-uh tee-eh) 锅贴儿
* meat pie
  xiànrbǐng (she-an bing) 馅儿饼
* fried leek dumplings
  jiǔcài hézi (gee-oh 'ts'-eye huh 'tz'-uh) 韭菜合子
* pancake
  jiānbing (gee-an bing) 煎饼

noodles
miàntiáo

steamed bread
with stuffings
bāozi

grilled chicken
shāo jī

beer
píjiǔ

fish stewed in
brown sauce
hóngshāo yú

spicy salt shrimp
jiāoyán xiā

roasted mutton
cubes on spit
yáng ròu chuàn

Let's speak
phrasebook
of mandarin
Chinese

Snacks & Dim Sum
Xiǎochī hé Diǎnxin (She-ow Chur Huh Dee-an Shin)
小吃和点心

* spring rolls
  chūnjuǎn (chun jew-an) 春卷
* hemp flowers
  máhuā (ma hwa) 麻花
* Chinese hamburger
  ròu jiā mó (row gee-ah moh-uh) 肉夹馍
* mutton shish kebab
  yáng ròu chuànr (yang row chew-an) 羊肉串儿
* 100-year egg
  pídàn (pee dan)皮蛋
* salted duck egg
  xián yā dàn (she-an yah dan) 咸鸭蛋
* stinky tofu (smelly tofu)
  chòu dòufu (choh doe foo) 臭豆腐
* custard bun
  nǎi huáng bāo ('n'eye huang bow) 奶黄包
* bean paste cake
  lǜ dòu gāo (lü doe gow) 绿豆糕
* sticky rice cakes
  nuòmǐ gāo (noah me gow) 糯米糕
* taro cake
  yùtou gāo (you toe gow) 芋头糕
* moon-cake
  yuèbing (you-eh bing) 月饼

* rice dumpling
  zòngzi ('tz'-ong 'tz'-uh) 粽子
* candied haws on a stick
  táng húlu (tang hoo lu) 糖葫芦

Drinks   Yǐnliào (Yin Lee-ow) 饮料

* cola
  kělè (kuh luh) 可乐
* sprite
  xuě bì (shoe-ay bee) 雪碧
* lemonade
  níngméng shuǐ (ning meng 'sh'-way) 柠檬水
* fruit juice
  shuǐguǒ zhī ('sh'-way go-uh jur) 水果汁
* apple juice
  píngguǒ zhī (ping go-uh jur) 苹果汁
* orange juice
  chéng zhī (chung jur) 橙汁
* mineral water
  kuàngquánshuǐ ('qu'-ang chew-an) 矿泉水
* milk
  niúnǎi (knee-oh 'n'eye) 牛奶
* cocoa
  rè qiǎokèlì (ruh chee-ow kuh lee) 热巧克力

Let's
speak
phrasebook
of mandarin
Chinese

* coffee
  kāfēi (ka fay) 咖啡
* black coffee
  qīng kāfēi (ching ka fay) 清咖啡
* white coffee
  níunǎi kāfēi (knee-oh 'n'eye ka fay) 牛奶咖啡
* coffee with cream and sugar
  jiā nǎi jiā táng de kāfēi
  (knee-oh 'n'eye gee-ah tang duh ka fay) 加奶加糖的咖啡
* instant coffee
  sùróng kāfēi (sue rong ka fay) 速溶咖啡
* soybean milk
  dòujiāng (doe gee-ang) 豆浆
* yogurt
  suānnǎi (sue-an 'n'eye) 酸奶
* tea
  chá (chah) 茶
* green tea
  lǜchá (lü chah) 绿茶
* black tea
  hóngchá (hong chah) 红茶
* jasmine tea
  mòlì huā chá (moh-uh lee hwa chah) 茉莉花茶

Alcoholic Drinks   Jiǔ (Gee-oh) 酒

* liquor
  báijiǔ (buy gee-oh) 白酒
* beer
  píjiǔ (pee gee-oh) 啤酒
* draught beer
  zhāpí (zhah pee) 扎啤
* light beer
  dàn píjiǔ (dan pee gee-oh) 淡啤酒
* shaoxing wine
  shàoxīngjiǔ (sh-ow shing gee-oh) 绍兴酒
* yellow wine
  huángjiǔ (huang gee-oh) 黄酒
* white wine
  bái pútáojiǔ (buy poo tow gee-oh) 白葡萄酒
* red wine
  hóng pútáojiǔ (hong poo tow gee-oh) 红葡萄酒
* champagne
  xiāngbīn (she-ang bin) 香槟
* whisky
  wēishìjì (way sure gee) 威士忌
* brandy
  báilándì (buy lan dee) 白兰地
* rum
  lán mǔ jiǔ (lan moo gee-oh) 兰姆酒

Let's
speak
phrasebook
of mandarin
Chinese

* cocktail
  jīwěijiǔ (gee way gee-oh) 鸡尾酒
* martini
  mǎ dīng ní jiǔ (ma ding knee gee-oh) 马丁尼酒
* tequila
  lóng shé lán jiǔ (long shuh lan gee-oh) 龙舌兰酒
* cider
  píngguǒ jiǔ (ping go-uh gee-oh) 苹果酒
* vodka
  fútèjiā (foo tuh gee-ah) 伏特加
* gin fizz
  dù sōng zǐ jiǔ (doo song 'tz'-uh gee-oh) 杜松子酒

Dessert Tiándiǎn (Tee-an Dee-an) 甜点

* cake
  dàngāo (dan gow) 蛋糕
* cream cake
  nǎiyóu dàngāo ('n'eye yoh dan gow) 奶油蛋糕
* pie
  xiànrbǐng (she-an bing) 馅儿饼
* ice-cream
  bīngqílín (bing chee lin) 冰淇淋
* vanilla ice-cream
  xiāng cǎo bīngqílín

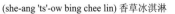

(she-ang 'ts'-ow bing chee lin) 香草冰淇淋

* chocolate ice-cream

qiǎokèlì bīngqílín

(chee-ow kuh lee bing chee lin) 巧克力冰淇淋

ice-cream
bīngqílín

cider
píng guǒ jiǔ

cake
dàngāo

pie
xiànrbǐng

Let's
speak
phrasebook
of mandarin
Chinese

PART 6

Shopping
Gòuwù (Goh Woo) 购物

Shops and Stores
Shāngdiàn (Shang Dee-an) 商店

1. **Where is the nearest ...?**
   Zuìjìn de ... zài nǎr?
   ('tz'-way gin đuh ... 'tz'-eye na?) 最近的 ... 在哪儿？

2. **I'd like to go to ....**
   Wǒ xiǎng qù ... (Wuh she-ang chew ...) 我想去 ...

3. **It there a (n) ... near here?**
   Zhèr fùjìn yǒu ... ma?
   (Juh foo gin yoh ... ma?) 这儿附近有 ... 吗？

---

* antique shop
  gǔdǒng diàn (goo dong dee-an) 古董店

* shopping center
  gòuwù zhōngxīn (goh woo zhong shin) 购物中心

* department store
  bǎihuò shāngchǎng (buy huo shang chang) 百货商场

* supermarket
  chāoshì (chow sure) 超市

* market
  shìchǎng (sure chang) 市场
* wholesale market
  pīfā shìchǎng (pee fah sure chang) 批发市场
* bookstore
  shū diàn (shoe dee-an) 书店
* flower shop
  huā diàn (hwa dee-an) 花店
* jewelry store
  zhūbǎo diàn (jew bow dee-an) 珠宝店
* video shop
  yīnxiàng shāngdiàn (yin she-ang shang dee-an)
  音像商店
* souvenir shop
  jìniànpǐn shāngdiàn (gee knee-an pin shang dee-an)
  纪念品商店

4. **Excuse me, where can I find some chocolate?**
   Qǐng wèn nǎr yǒu mài qiǎokèlì de?
   (Ching when na yoh my chee-ow kuh lee duh?)
   请问哪儿有卖巧克力的？

5. **Does the shop closes at 6:00 pm?**
   Shāngdiàn xiàwǔ liù diǎn guān mén, shì ma?
   (Shang dee-an she-ah woo lee-oh dee-an gu-on men,
   sure ma?) 商店下午6点关门，是吗？

外国人学说中国话

Let's
speak
phrasebook
of mandarin
Chinese

PART 6

Buying Gòumǎi (Goh My) 购买

1. **Excuse me, where can I find a shopping cart?**
   Qǐng wèn, nǎr néng zhǎo dào shǒutuīchē?
   (Ching when na neng 'j'-ow dow 'sh'-way too-ay chuh?) 请问，哪儿能找到手推车？

2. **May I see these silk ties?**
   Wǒ néng kànkan zhèxiē sī zhì lǐngdài ma?
   (Wuh neng can can juh she-ay si jur ling die ma?)
   我能看看这些丝质领带吗？

3. **Can I have a look?**
   Wǒ néng kànkan ma? (Wuh neng can can ma?)
   我能看看吗？

4. **Please show me some pure silk blouses.**
   Qǐng ná jǐ jiàn zhēn sī chènshān gěi wǒ kànkan, hǎo ma? (Ching na gee gee-an jen si chen shan gay wuh can can, how ma?)
   请拿几件真丝衬衫给我看看，好吗？

5. **That needlework is beautiful!**
   Duō hǎo de xiù gōng a!
   (Doh-uh how duh she-oh gong a!) 多好的绣工啊！

Clothes Yīfu ('e' Foo) 衣服

* attire | fúzhuāng (foo jee-ang) 服装
* a hat | màozi (mao 'tz'-uh) 帽子
* a shirt | chènshān (chen shan) 衬衫
* a blouse | nǚ chènshān (nü chen shan) 女衬衫
* a jacket | shàngyī (shang 'e') 上衣
* a coat | wàitào (why tow) 外套
* a fur | pí yī (pee 'e') 皮衣
* a cheongsam | qípáo (chee pow) 旗袍
* a scarf | wéijīn (way gin) 围巾
* a tie | lǐngdài (ling die) 领带
* a pair of trousers | kùzi (koo 'tz'-uh) 裤子
* a belt | pí dài (pee die) 皮带
* stockings | wàzi (wah 'tz'-uh) 袜子
* shoes | xié (she-ay) 鞋
* leather shoes | pí xié (pee she-ay) 皮鞋
* a Chinese tunic suit
  zhōngshānzhuāng (zhong shan jee-ang) 中山装
* a Tang suit (traditional Chinese clothing)
  tángzhuāng (tang jee-ang) 唐装

6. Do you have any others?
   Hái yǒu bié de ma? (Hi yoh bee-eh duh ma?)
   还有别的吗？

7. Can I try it on?
   Wǒ kěyǐ shìchuān yī xià ma? (Wuh kuh 'e' sure chew-an 'e' she-ah ma?) 我可以试穿一下吗？

外国人学说中国话

Let's
speak
phrasebook
of mandarin
Chinese

PART 6

Measurements	Zhàngliáng ('j'-ang Lee-ang) 丈量
* size	chǐcùn (chur 'ts'-un) 尺寸
* extra large (XL)	tè dàhào (tuh da how) 特大号
* large (L)	dàhào (da how) 大号
* medium (M)	zhōng hào (zhong how) 中号
* small (S)	xiǎo hào (she-ow how) 小号
* short	duǎn (do-an) 短
* long	cháng (chang) 长
* tight	jǐn (gin) 紧
* loose	sōng (song) 松
* circumference	xiōngwéi (she-ong way) 胸围
* waist size	yāowéi (yow way) 腰围
* hipline	túnwéi (tun way) 臀围

8. Where is the fitting room?

Shìyījiān zài nǎr? (Sue 'e' gee-an 'tz'-eye na?)

试衣间在哪儿？

9. Do you have a mirror?

Yǒu jìngzi ma? (Yoh jing 'tz'-uh ma?)

有镜子吗？

10. I like this style, but I don't care for the color.

Wǒ xǐhuan zhè yàngshì, dàn bù xǐhuan zhè yánsè.

(Wuh she huan juh yang sure, dan boo she huan juh yan suh.) 我喜欢这样式，但不喜欢这颜色。

Color   Yánsè (Yan Suh) 颜色

* red
  hóngsè (hong suh) 红色
* wine red
  pútáojiǔ hóngsè (poo tow gee-oh hong suh) 葡萄酒红色
* scarlet
  shēn hóngsè (shen hong suh) 深红色
* pink
  fěnhóngsè (fen hong suh) 粉红色
* salmon pink
  qiǎn chéngsè (chee-an chung suh) 浅橙色
* orange
  chéngsè (chung suh) 橙色
* brown
  hèsè (huh suh) 褐色
* green
  lǜsè (lü suh) 绿色
* cyan
  qīng sè (ching suh) 青色
* blue
  lánsè (lan suh) 蓝色
* cobalt blue
  shēn lánsè (shen lan suh) 深蓝色
* olive green
  gǎnlǎnlǜ (gan lan lü) 橄榄绿
* navy blue
  zàngqīng sè ('tz'-ang ching suh) 藏青色
* mauve
  zǐhóngsè ('tz'-uh hong suh) 紫红色

外国人说中国话

* lavender
  dàn zǐsè (dan 'tz'-uh suh) 淡紫色
* white
  báisè (buy suh) 白色
* snowy white
  xuěbái sè (shoe-ay buy suh) 雪白色
* gray
  huīsè (hui suh) 灰色
* black
  hēisè (hay suh) 黑色
* yellow
  huángsè (huang suh) 黄色

11. **It's high quality.**
    Zhège zhìliàng hǎo.
    (Juh guh jur lee-ang how.)
    这个质量好。

I think I'll take it.
Wǒ jiù mǎi tā ba.

Souvenir	Jìniànpǐn (Gee Knee-an) 纪念品

* Chinese knot   zhōngguójié (zhong go-uh gee-ay) 中国结
* Cloisonné ware   jǐngtàilán (jing tye lan) 景泰蓝
* porcelain   cíqì ('ts'-uh chee) 瓷器
* wax printing   làrǎn (la ran) 蜡染
* embroider   cìxiù ('ts'-uh she-oh) 刺绣
* red porcelain   zǐshā ('tz'-uh sha) 紫砂
* paper-cut   jiǎnzhǐ (gee-an jur) 剪纸
* woodcarving   mùdiāo (moo dee-ow) 木雕
* root carving   gēndiāo (gen dee-ow) 根雕
* lacquerwork   qīqì (chee chee) 漆器

---

12. I think I'll take it.

Wǒ jiù mǎi tā ba. (Wuh gee-oh my ta ba.)
我就买它吧。

---

13. The coat fits me perfectly.

Zhè jiàn dàyī zhèng hé wǒ shēn. (Juh gee-an da 'e' jung huh wuh shen.) 这件大衣正合我身。

---

14. If this coat doesn't fit, may I bring it back later?

Rúguǒ zhè jiàn yīfu bù héshēn, wǒ kěyǐ ná huílái tuì huò ma?

(Roo go-uh juh gee-an 'e' foo boo huh shen, wuh kuh 'e' na hui lie too-ay huo ma?)

如果这件衣服不合身，我可以拿回来退货吗？

15. I'd like to buy two boxes of egg yolk mooncakes.

Wǒ xiǎng mǎi liǎng hé dànhuáng yuèbing.

(Wuh she-ang my lee-ang huh dan huang you-eh bing.) 我想买两盒蛋黄月饼。

---

16. Please weigh it for me.

Qǐng bāng wǒ chēng yī xià. (Ching bang wuh chung 'e' she-ah.) 请帮我称一下。

---

17. Will you wrap them separately?

Qǐng nǐ gěi wǒ fēnkāi bāozhuāng.

(Ching knee gay wuh fen 'k'-eye bow jee-ang.) 请你给我分开包装。

---

18. Do you have platinum jewelry?

Nǐmen yǒu báijīn shìpǐn ma? (Kne men yoh buy gin sure pin ma?) 你们有白金饰品吗？

Jewelry Zhūbǎo Shìwù
(Jew Bow Sure Woo) 珠宝饰物

* a necklace	xiàngliàn (she-ang lee-an)	项链
* a ring	jièzhi (gee-ay jur)	戒指
* a bracelet	shǒuzhuó (show joe-uh)	手镯
* earrings	ěrhuán (are huan)	耳环
* a brooch	xiōngzhēn (she-ong jen)	胸针
* headdress flowers	tóu huā (toe hwa)	头花
* pure gold	chún jīn (chun gin)	纯金
* sterling silver	jiǔ-èr-wǔ yín (gee-oh are woo yin)	925银

* genuine diamond   zhēn zuàn (jen zoo-an) 真钻
* gemstone   bǎoshí (bow sure) 宝石
* ruby   hóngbǎoshí (hong bow sure) 红宝石
* sapphire   lánbǎoshí (lan bow sure) 蓝宝石
* emerald   lǜ bǎo shí (lǖ bow sure) 绿宝石
* jade   yù (you) 玉

19. What's this material?

Zhè shì shénme cáiliào de? (Juh sure shen muh 'ts'-eye lee-ow duh?) 这是什么材料的？

20. Where was this product made?

Zhè shì nǎlǐ shēngchǎn de? (Juh sure na lee sheng chan duh?) 这是哪里生产的？

21. Are there English instructions with it?

Yǒu yīngwén shuōmíngshū ma? (Yoh ying when show-uh ming shoe ma?) 有英文说明书吗？

Material Cáiliào ('ts'-eye Lee-ow) 材料

* cotton   mián zhì (me-an jur) 棉制
* silk   zhēnsī (jen si) 真丝
* filamentous sī zhì (si jur) 丝质
* lace   lěi sī (lay si) 蕾丝
* pure wool   chún yángmáo (chun yang mao) 纯羊毛
* mohair   mǎhǎimáo (ma hi mao) 马海毛

外国人学说中国话

* linen	yàmá (yah ma) 亚麻
* cashmere	yángróng (yang rong) 羊绒
* down-filled	yǔróng (you rong) 羽绒
* polyester	dílún (dee lun) 涤纶
* nylon	nílóng (knee long) 尼龙
* leather	pígé (pee guh) 皮革
* artificial leather	rénzàogé (ren tzow guh) 人造革
* rubber	xiàngjiāo (she-ang gee-ow) 橡胶

22. **I'm interested in Chinese antiques.**

Wǒ duì zhōngguó gǔdǒng hěn gǎn xìngqù.

(Wuh 'd'-way zhong go-uh goo dong hen gan shing chew.)

我对中国古董很感兴趣。

23. **Are these antiques and Chinese paintings genuine or reproductions?**

Zhèxiē gǔdǒng hé zhōngguóhuà shì zhēnpǐn háishì fùzhì pǐn?

(Juh she-ay goo dong huh zhong go-uh hwa sure jen pin hi sure foo jur pin?)

这些古董和中国画是真品还是复制品？

24. **Will I have problems with customs?**

Guò hǎiguān huì yǒu wèntí ma?

(Go-uh hi gu-on hui yoh when tee ma?)

过海关会有问题吗？

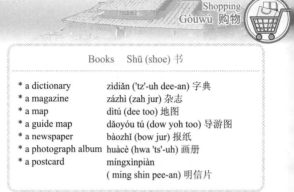

Books   Shū (shoe) 书

* a dictionary	zìdiǎn ('tz'-uh dee-an) 字典
* a magazine	zázhì (zah jur) 杂志
* a map	dìtú (dee too) 地图
* a guide map	dǎoyóu tú (dow yoh too) 导游图
* a newspaper	bàozhǐ (bow jur) 报纸
* a photograph album	huàcè (hwa 'ts'-uh) 画册
* a postcard	míngxìnpiàn
	(ming shin pee-an) 明信片

Asking about Price and Bargaining
Xún Jià hé Kǎn Jià (Sh-une Gee-ah Huh
Can Gee-ah) 询价和砍价

1. **How much is this mobile phone?**
Zhège shǒujī duōshao qián? (Juh guh show gee doh-
uh sh-ow chee-an?) 这个手机多少钱?

2. **How much do you want?**
Nǐ yào duōshao?
(Knee yow doh-uh sh-ow?) 你要多少?

* China Unicom	zhōngguó lián tōng
	(zhong go-uh lee-an tong) 中国联通
* China Mobile	zhōngguó yídòng
	(zhong go-uh 'e' dong) 中国移动

外国人学说中国话

Let's
speak
Phrasebook
of mandarin
Chinese

PART 6

* chord	héxián (huh she-an)	和弦
* earphone	ěrjī (are gee)	耳机
* model	xínghào (shing how)	型号
* multimedia message	cǎixìn ('ts'-eye shin)	彩信
* phone fee	huàfèi (hwa fay)	话费
* recharge	chōngzhí kǎ (chong jur ka)	充值卡
* ring tone	língshēng (ling sheng)	铃声
* screen	píngmù (ping moo)	屏幕
* storage capacity	cúnchǔ róngliàng ('ts'-un chew rong lee-ang)	存储容量
* use's guide	shuōmíngshū (show-uh ming shoe)	说明书
* volume	yīnliàng (yin lee-ang)	音量
* weight	zhòngliàng (zhong lee-ang)	重量
* warranty	bǎo xiū (bow she-oh)	保修
* call duration	tōnghuà shíjiān (tong hwa sure gee-an) 通话时间	

3. **Do you have anything cheaper?**
   Yǒu piányi de ma? (Yoh pee-an 'e' duh ma?)
   有便宜的吗？

4. **It's too expensive.**
   Tài guì le. (Tye 'g'way luh.) 太贵了。

5. **No wonder it's so expensive.**
   Guàibu de zhème guì. (Gu-eye boo duh juh muh 'g' way.) 怪不得这么贵。

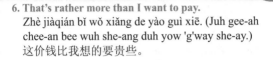

6. **That's rather more than I want to pay.**

   Zhè jiàqián bǐ wǒ xiǎng de yào guì xiē. (Juh gee-ah chee-an bee wuh she-ang duh yow 'g'way she-ay.)

   这价钱比我想的要贵些。

---

7. **It's good material, but it's a little on the expensive side.**

   Liàozi hǎo shì hǎo, jiùshì guì le xiē. (Lee-ow 'tz'-uh how sure how, gee-oh sure 'g'way luh she-ay.)

   料子好是好，就是贵了些。

---

8. **Can you come down a little?**

   Nǐ néng piányi yī diǎnrmài ma? (Knee neng pee-an 'e' 'e' dee-an my ma?) 你能便宜一点儿卖吗？

---

9. **If you lower the price, next time I'll come back.**

   Rúguǒ piányi diǎnr, xià cì wǒ hái lái. (Roo go-uh pee-an 'e' dee-an, she-ah 'ts'-uh wuh hi lie.)

   如果便宜点儿，下次我还来。

I think 100 *yuan* is still too much. How about 60 *yuan*?
Wǒ juéde yī-bǎi yuán háishì guì, liù-shí yuán xíng ma?

外国人说中国话

10. I think 100 *yuan* is still too much. How about 60 *yuan*?

Wǒ juéde yī-bǎi yuán háishì guì, liù-shí yuán xíng ma? (Wuh jew-ay duh 'e' buy you-an hi sure 'g'way, lee-oh sure you-an shing ma?)

我觉得100元还是贵，60元行吗？

11. I need to think about it for a moment.

Wǒ kǎolǜ yī xià. (Wuh cow lu-ay 'e' she-ah.)

我考虑一下。

12. It's a real bargain.

Zhè shì zhēnzhèng de piányi huò. (Juh sure jen jung duh pee-an 'e' huo.) 这是真正的便宜货。

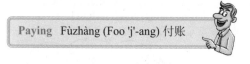

Paying Fùzhàng (Foo 'j'-ang) 付账

1. What's the total cost?

Yīgòng duōshao qián?

('e' gong doh-uh sh-ow chee-an?) 一共多少钱？

2. Where do I pay?

Zài nǎr fùzhàng? ('tz' na foo'j'-ang?) 在哪儿付账？

3. I don't have any cash with me.

Wǒ méiyǒu xiànjīn le. (Wuh may yoh she-an gin luh.) 我没有现金了。

4. **Does this shop accept cheques or credit cards?**
   Zhèr néng yòng zhīpiào huò xìnyòngkǎ fùzhàng ma? (Juh neng yong jur pee-ow huo shin yong ka foo 'j'-ang ma?) 这儿能用支票或信用卡付账吗？

5. **Could you please give me the receipt?**
   Qǐng gěi wǒ kāi zhāng fāpiào. (Ching gay wuh 'k'-eye 'j'-ang fah pee-ow.) 请给我开张发票。

6. **I've no small change.**
   Wǒ méiyǒu língqián. (Wuh may yoh ling chee-an.) 我没有零钱。

What's the total cost?
Yīgòng duōshao qián?

Parties
Jùhuì (Jew Hui) 聚会

Making an Invitation
Yāoqǐng (Yow Ching) 邀请

1. I would like to invite you to dinner tonight, are you free?

Wǎnshàng xiǎng qǐng nǐ chīfàn, nǐ yǒu shíjiān ma?

(Wan shang she-ang ching knee chur fan, knee yoh sure gee-an ma?)

晚上想请你吃饭，你有时间吗？

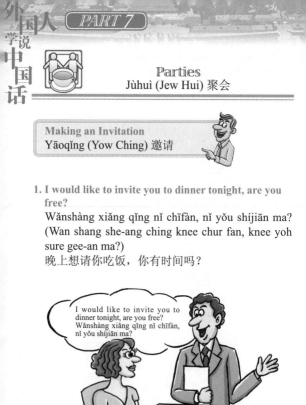

I would like to invite you to dinner tonight, are you free?
Wǎnshàng xiǎng qǐng nǐ chīfàn, nǐ yǒu shíjiān ma?

2. **We're holding a party on the weekend, can you come?**
Zhōumò wǒmen yǒu ge jùhuì, nǐ néng lái ma?
(Joe moh-uh wuh men yoh guh jew hui, knee neng lie ma?) 周末我们有个聚会，你能来吗？

3. **We're having a party outside the house tonight. Do you want to join us?**
Wǒmen jīn wǎn jǔbàn hùwài jùhuì, nǐ lái ma?
(Wuh men gin wan jew ban who why jew hui, knee lie ma?)
我们今晚举办户外聚会，你来吗？

4. **I'll be there.**
Wǒ yīdìng qù. (Wuh 'e' ding chew.)
我一定去。

5. **It's a deal.**
Hǎo, yī yán wéi dìng.
(How, 'e' yan way ding.)
好，一言为定。

6. **Thanks. That's very kind of you.**
Xièxie, zhēn shì tài máfán nǐ le.
(She-ay she-ay, jen sure tye ma fan knee luh.)
谢谢，真是太麻烦你了。

7. **I am sorry. I can't go.**
Zhēn duìbuqǐ, wǒ qù bu liǎo. (Jen 'd'-way boo   chee, **Let's
speak**
phrasebook
of mandarin
Chinese

wuh chew boo lee-ow.)
真对不起，我去不了。

8. It's extremely kind of you to offer, but I happen to have something I need to deal with.

Xièxie nǐ de hǎoyì, kěshì wǒ gānghǎo yǒu diǎn shìr.

(She-ay she-ay knee duh how 'e', kuh sure wuh gang how yoh dee-an sure.)

谢谢你的好意，可是我刚好有点事儿。

9. Some other time, perhaps.

Gǎi tiān ba. (Guy tee-an ba.) 改天吧。

10. Let's make it Sunday.

Nà jiù xīngqītiān ba.

(Na gee-oh shing chee tee-an ba.)

那就星期天吧。

Welcome Huānyíng (Huan Ying) 欢迎

1. Welcome to my home.

Huānyíng lái wǒ jiā. (Huan ying lie wuh gee-ah.)
欢迎来我家。

2. Come in and make yourself at home.

Qǐng jìn, bié kèqi. (Ching gin, bee-eh kuh chee.)
请进，别客气。

---

3. Sorry, I'm late.
Duìbuqǐ, wǒ lái wǎn le.
('d'-way boo chee, wuh lie wan luh.)
对不起，我来晚了。

---

4. Glad to meet you. Come in, please.
Jiàn dào nǐ hěn gāoxìng, qǐng jìnlái .
(Gee-an dow knee hen gow shing, ching gin lie.)
见到你很高兴，请进来。

---

5. Take a seat please.
Qǐng zuò. (Ching 'z'-oh-uh.) 请坐。

Welcome to my home.
Huānyíng lái wǒ jiā.

Let's
speak
phrasebook
of mandarin
Chinese

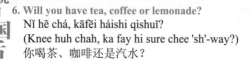

6. Will you have tea, coffee or lemonade?

Nǐ hē chá, kāfēi háishi qìshuǐ?

(Knee huh chah, ka fay hi sure chee 'sh'-way?)

你喝茶、咖啡还是汽水？

7. Thank you for your kind hospitality.

Xièxie nǐ de shèngqíng kuǎndài.

(She-ay she-ay knee duh sheng ching kuan die.)

谢谢你的盛情款待。

8. Let me show you around the house.

Wǒ dài nǐ cānguān yī xià.

(Wuh die knee 'ts'-an gu-on 'e' she-ah.)

我带你参观一下。

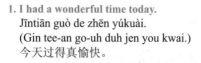

Saying Goodbye and Farewell

Dàobié hé Sòngxíng (Dow Bee-eh Huh
Song Shing) 道别和送行

1. I had a wonderful time today.

Jīntiān guò de zhēn yúkuài.

(Gin tee-an go-uh duh jen you kwai.)

今天过得真愉快。

2. Don't bother to see me out.

Qǐng liúbù. (Ching lee-oh boo.) 请留步。

3. **Take care.**
Màn zǒu. (Man tzoh.) 慢走。

4. **I can not go any further.**
Bù yuǎn sòng le. (Boo you-an song luh.)
不远送了。

5. **Bon Voyage!**
Yīlù píng'ān! ('e' lu ping an!)
一路平安！

6. **Come and see us again soon.**
Yǒu kōngr zài lái zuòzuo.
(Yoh kong 'tz'-eye lie 'z'-oh-uh 'z'-oh-uh.)
有空儿再来坐坐。

7. **Have a pleasant journey!**
Yīlù shùnfēng! ('e' lu shun feng!) 一路顺风！

TIPS

In China, when visiting someone, we also need to make arrangements, just like that in western countries. Before visiting someone, Chinese often make plans. On one hand, they don't want to disturb others or bring any inconvenience to them. On the other hand, making plans helps others arrange their time better.

Let's
speak
phrasebook
of mandarin
Chinese

Lifestyle Services
Shēnghuó Fúwù
(Sheng Huo Foo Woo) 生活服务

Leisure Yúlè (You Luh) 娱乐

1. Are you free tonight?

Jīntiān wǎnshang yǒu kòngr ma? (Gin tee-an wan shang yoh kong ma?) 今天晚上有空儿吗？

2. Can you recommend a …?

Nǐ néng tuījiàn yī ge … ma? (Knee neng too-ay gee-an 'e' guh … ma?) 你能推荐一个 … 吗？

* bar
  jiǔbā (gee-oh ba) 酒吧
* Internet bar
  wǎngbā (wang ba) 网吧
* karaoke club
  kǎ-lā OK jiǔbā (ka la OK gee-oh ba) 卡拉OK酒吧
* teahouse
  cháguǎn (chah gu-on) 茶馆
* café
  kāfēitīng (ka fay ting) 咖啡厅

* disco
dísikē wǔtīng (dee si kuh woo ting) 迪斯科舞厅
* dance hall
wǔtīng (woo ting) 舞厅
* nightclub
yèzǒnghuì (yeh 'tz'-ong hui) 夜总会
* theater
jùyuàn (jew you-an) 剧院
* cinema
diànyǐngyuàn (dee-an ying you-an) 电影院
* massage parlor
ànmó yuàn (an moh-uh you-an) 按摩院

---

3. I'm sure you'll have fun at the party tonight.

Nǐ zài jīn wǎn de wǎnhuì shàng yīdìng huì wánr de
hěn kāixīn. (Knee 'tz'-eye gin wan duh wan hui shang
'e' ding hui wan duh hen 'k'-eye shin.)
你在今晚的晚会上一定会玩儿得很开心。

---

4. Can I get you a drink?

Wǒ néng qǐng nǐ hē diǎnr dōngxi ma?
(Wuh neng ching knee huh dee-an dong she ma?)
我能请你喝点儿东西吗？

---

5. I want to sing at a karaoke club next.

Jiē xiàlái, wǒ xiǎng qù kǎ-lā OK jiǔbā chànggē.
(Gee-ay she-ah lie wuh she-ang chew ka la OK gee-

外国人学说中国话

oh ba chang guh.)
接下来，我想去卡拉OK酒吧唱歌。

---

* song
  gēqǔ (guh chew) 歌曲
* lyrics
  gēcí (guh 'ts'-uh) 歌词
* microphone
  màikèfēng (my kuh feng) 麦克风
* mike
  huàtǒng (hwa tong) 话筒
* subtitles
  zìmù ('tz'-uh moo) 字幕
* volume
  yīnliàng (yin lee-ang) 音量
* an expert in
  náshǒu (na show) 拿手
* tone-deaf
  wǔyīn bù quán (woo yin boo chew-an) 五音不全
* out of tune
  zǒudiàor (tzoh dee-ow) 走调儿

---

6. Would you like to join us?

Nǐ xiǎng yīqǐ lái ma?
(Knee she-ang 'e' chee lie ma?) 你想一起来吗？

---

7. Where do you want to meet?

Wǒmen zài nǎr jiànmiàn? (Wuh men 'tz'-eye na ge-an me-an?) 我们在哪儿见面？

8. Do you like Beijing Opera?

Nǐ xǐhuan jīngjù ma?
(Knee she huan jing jew ma?) 你喜欢京剧吗?

Beijing Opera   Jīngjù (Jing Jew) 京剧

* Biejing Opera fan
  jīngjù piàoyǒu (jing jew pee-ow yoh) 京剧票友
* facial makeup
  liǎnpǔ (lee-an poo) 脸谱
* male character
  shēngjué (sheng jew-ay) 生角
* female character
  dànjué (dan jew-ay) 旦角
* painted-face character huāliǎn (hwa lee-an) 花脸
* buffoon / clown
  chǒujué (choh jew-ay) 丑角
* supporting role
  pǎolóngtào (pow long tow) 跑龙套

9. The opera was fabulous.

Zhè bù gējù hěn jīngcǎi. (Juh boo guh jew hen jing 'ts'-eye.) 这部歌剧很精彩。

10. The second show starts at 8 o'clock.

Dì èr chǎng yǎnchū wǎnshàng bā diǎnzhōng kāishǐ. (Dee are chang yan chew wan shang ba dee-an zhong 'k'-eye sure.)

PART 8

Let's
speak
phrasebook
of mandarin
Chinese

第二场演出晚上8点钟开始。

---

11. I've seen that film before.

Nà bù diànyǐng wǒ yǐqián kànguo.

(Na boo dee-an ying wuh 'e' chee-an can go-uh.)

那部电影我以前看过。

---

12. I'm queuing to buy tickets.

Wǒ zhèngzài páiduì mǎi piào.

(Wuh jung 'tz'-eye pie 'd'-way my pee-ow.)

我正在排队买票。

---

13. The horror film on television last night scared the hell out of me.

Zuó wǎn diànshì shàng fàngyìng de kǒngbù piàn bǎ wǒ xiàhuàile. ('z'-oh-uh wan dee-an sure shang fong ying duh kong boo pee-an ba wuh she-ah h-why luh.) 昨晚电视上放映的恐怖片把我吓坏了。

---

* cartoon	dònghuàpiànr (dong hwa pee-an)	动画片儿
* kung-fu movie	gōngfu piàn (gong foo pee-an)	功夫片
* horror film	kǒngbù piàn (kong boo pee-an)	恐怖片
* drama	yánqíng piàn (yan ching pee-an)	言情片
* comedy	xǐjù piàn (she jew pee-an)	喜剧片
* musical	gēwǔ piàn (guh woo pee-an)	歌舞片
* series	liánxùjù (lee-an shoe jew)	连续剧
* soap opera	féizàojù (fay tzow jew)	肥皂剧

14. I'm not good at dancing.

Wǒ tiàowǔ yīdiǎnr yě bù xíng.

(Wuh tee-ow woo 'e' dee-an yeh boo shing.)

我跳舞一点儿也不行。

* ballet
  bāléiwǔ (ba lay woo) 芭蕾舞
* belly dancing
  dùpí wǔ (do pee woo) 肚皮舞
* break dancing
  pīliwǔ (pee lee woo) 霹雳舞
* chacha
  qiàqià (chee-ah chee-ah) 恰恰
* Chinese traditional folk dance
  Zhōngguó chuántǒng mínzú wǔ (zhong go-uh chew-an tong min tzoo woo) 中国传统民族舞
* Latin dance
  lādīngwǔ (la ting woo) 拉丁舞
* modern dance
  xiàndàiwǔ (she-an die woo) 现代舞
* rumba
  lúnbā (lun ba) 伦巴
* street dancing
  jiēwǔ (gee-ay woo) 街舞
* tap
  tītàwǔ (tee ta woo) 踢踏舞
* tango
  tàngē (tan guh) 探戈

外国人学说中国话

15. Thanks for a nice evening.

Jīn wǎn guò de zhēn yúkuài, xièxie nǐ le. (Gin wan go-uh duh jen you kwai, she-ay she-ay knee luh.)

今晚过得真愉快，谢谢你了。

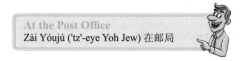

At the Post Office

Zài Yóujú ('tz'-eye Yoh Jew) 在邮局

---

1. How much is the postage for an airmail letter to Canada?

Jì wǎng Jiānádà de hángkōngxìn yào duōshao yóufèi? (Gee wang gee-ah na da duh hong kong shin yow doh-uh sh-ow yoh fay?)

寄往加拿大的航空信要多少邮费？

---

2. How much will it cost to send it by express mail?

Jì tèkuàixìn yào duōshao qián?

(Gee tuh kwai shin yow doh-uh sh-ow chee-an?)

寄特快信要多少钱？

---

3. What's the surcharge on this express parcel?

Zhège kuài yóu bāoguǒ de éwài yóuzī shì duōshao? (Juh guh kwai yoh bow go-uh duh are why yoh 'tz'-uh sure doh-uh sh-ow?)

这个快邮包裹的额外邮资是多少？

---

* post office
  yóujú (yoh jew) 邮局
* branch post office
  yóuzhèng zhī jú (yoh jung jur jew) 邮政支局
* local
  běnbù (ben boo) 本埠
* mail box
  xìnxiāng (shin she-ang) 信箱
* postal code
  yóuzhèng biānmǎ (yoh jung bee-an ma) 邮政编码
* postman
  yóudìyuán (yoh dee you-an) 邮递员
* stamp
  yóupiào (yoh pee-ow) 邮票
* postage
  yóuzī (yoh 'tz'-uh) 邮资
* postage paid
  yóuzī yǐ fù (yoh 'tz'-uh 'e' foo) 邮资已付
* postmark
  yóuchuō (yoh choh-uh) 邮戳
* delivery
  dìsòng (dee song) 递送
* mail a letter
  jìxìn (gee shin) 寄信
* sender
  fā xìn rén (fah shin ren) 发信人
* consignee
  shōu huò rén (show huo ren) 收货人
* addressee
  shōu jiàn rén (show gee-an ren) 收件人

外国人学说中国话

Let's speak
phrasebook of mandarin Chinese

* payee
  shōu kuǎn rén (show kuan ren) 收款人
* envelope
  xìnfēng (shin feng) 信封
* writing pad
  xìnzhǐ (shin jur) 信纸
* address
  dìzhǐ (dee jur) 地址
* heading
  biāotí (bee-ow tee) 标题
* date
  rìqī (ree chee) 日期
* postscript (P.S)
  fùbǐ (foo bee) 附笔
* please forward
  qǐng zhuǎnfā (ching jew-an fah) 请转发
* express mail
  kuàixìn (kwai shin) 快信
* registered letter
  guàhào xìn (guah how shin) 挂号信
* ordinary mail
  píngxìn (ping shin) 平信
* airmail
  hángkōng yóujiàn (hong kong yoh gee-an) 航空邮件
* postcard
  míngxìnpiàn (ming shin pee-an) 明信片
* return receipt
  huízhí (hui jur) 回执
* postal order
  yóuzhèng huìpiào (yoh jung hui pee-ao) 邮政汇票

* printed matter
  yìnshuāpǐn (yin shoe-ah pin) 印刷品
* EMS
  tèkuàizhuāndì (tuh kwai jew-an dee) 特快专递
* Fed Ex
  liánbāng kuàidì (lee-an bang kwai dee) 联邦快递

4. I want to mail this parcel to New York.

Wǒ xiǎng bǎ zhè bāoguǒ jì wǎng Niǔyuē.
(Wuh she-ang ba juh bow go-uh gee wang knee-oh you-eh.) 我想把这包裹寄往纽约。

5. How long will it take for this parcel to arrive?

Zhè ge bāoguǒ duō jiǔ néng jì dào?
(Juh guh bow go-uh doh-uh jee-oh neng gee dow?) 这个包裹多久能寄到？

6. I want to send an EMS.

Wǒ jì tèkuài zhuāndì.
(Wuh gee tuh kwai jew-an dee.) 我寄特快专递。

7. I'd like to pick up my package. This is the notice.

Wǒ xiǎng qǔ wǒ de bāoguǒ. Zhè shì tōngzhī dān.
(Wuh she-ang chew wuh duh bow go-uh. Juh sure tong jur dan.) 我想取我的包裹。这是通知单。

8. Could you please pack this for me?

外国人学说中国话

Nǐ néng bāng wǒ bāozhuāng yī xià ma?
(Knee neng bang wuh bow jee-ang 'e' she-ah ma?)
你能帮我包装一下吗？

At the Bank
Zài Yínháng ('tz'-eye Yin Hong) 在银行

1. When will the bank open?

Yínháng jǐ diǎn kāi mén?
(Yin hong gee dee-an 'k'-eye men?) 银行几点开门？

Bank   Yínháng (Yin Hong) 银行

* Bank of China (BC)
  Zhōngguó Yínháng (zhong go-uh yin hong) 中国银行
* Industrial and Commercial Bank of China (ICBC)
  Zhōngguó Gōngshāng Yínháng
  (zhong go-uh gong shang yin hong) 中国工商银行
* China Construction Bank (CCB)
  Zhōngguó Jiànshè Yínháng
  (zhong go-uh gee-an shuh yin hong) 中国建设银行
* Agricultural Bank of China (ABC)
  Zhōngguó Nóngyè Yínháng
  (zhong go-uh nong yeh yin hong) 中国农业银行
* Bank of Beijing (BB)
  Běijīng Yínháng (bay jing yin hong) 北京银行
* Bank of Communications (BC)

Jiāotōng Yínháng (gee-ow tong yin hong) 交通银行
* China Merchants Bank (CMB)
  Zhāoshāng Yínháng ('j'-ow shang yin hong) 招商银行
* ATM
  zìdòng tíkuǎnjī ('tz'-uh dong tee kuan gee) 自动提款机
* banking hours
  yíngyè shíjiān (ying yeh sure gee-an) 营业时间
* foreign exchange
  wàihuì (why hui) 外汇
* false money
  jiǎbì (gee-ah bee) 假币

2. I'd like to deposit 2,000 *yuan* into my bank account.

Wǒ xiǎng zài wǒ de hùtóu shàng cún liǎngqiān yuán.
(Wuh she-ang 'tz'-eye wuh duh who toe shang 'ts'-un
lee-ang chee-an you-an.)
我想在我的户头上存2000元。

Deposit   Cúnkuǎn ('ts'-un Kuan) 存款

* savings account
  Chǔxù cúnkuǎn (chew shoe 'ts'-un kuan) 储蓄存款
* current account
  huóqī cúnkuǎn (huo chee 'ts'-un kuan) 活期存款
* fixed account
  dìngqī cúnkuǎn (ding chee 'ts'-un kuan) 定期存款
* fixed deposit installments
  líng cún zhěng qǔ (ling 'ts'-un jung chew) 零存整取

3. **I'd like to open a bank account.**

Wǒ xiǎng kāi yī ge zhànghù. (Wuh she-ang 'k'-eye 'e' guh 'j'-ang who.) 我想开一个账户。

* checking account
  zhīpiào zhànghù (jur pee-ow 'j'-ang who) 支票账户
* deposit receipt
  cúndān ('ts'-un dan) 存单
* bank book
  cúnzhé ('ts'-un jur) 存折
* credit card
  xìnyòngkǎ (shin yong ka) 信用卡
* password
  mìmǎ (me ma) 密码
* signature
  qiānmíng (chee-an ming) 签名
* depositor
  cúnhù ('ts'-un who) 存户

4. **Is there a minimum for the first deposit?**

Dì yī cì chǔxù yǒu zuì dī xiàn'é ma? (Dee 'e' 'ts'-uh chew shoe yoh 'tz'-way dee she-an are ma?) 第一次储蓄有最低限额吗？

5. **What's the interest rate for …?**

… de lìlǜ shì duōshao? (… duh lee lü sure doh-uh show?) … 的利率是多少？

6. I want to withdraw 500 EUR.

Wǒ qǔ wǔbǎi ōuyuán.

(Wuh chew woo buy oh you-an.) 我取500欧元。

7. Could you give me some …?

Néng bāng wǒ huàn diǎnr … ma? (Neng bang wuh huan dee-an … ma?) 能帮我换点儿 … 吗？

Currency   Bìzhǒng (Bee Zhong) 币种

* Renminbi (RMB)
  rénmínbì (ren min bee) 人民币
* U.S. dollar
  měiyuán (may you-an) 美元
* English pound
  yīngbàng (ying bang) 英镑
* Euro (EUR)
  ōuyuán (oh you-an) 欧元
* Japanese yen
  rìyuán (reee you-an) 日元
* Hong Kong dollar
  gǎngbì (gang bee) 港币

8. I'd like to cash this money order.

Wǒ xiǎng duìxiàn zhè zhāng huìkuǎndān.

(Wuh she-ang 'd'-way she-an juh 'j'-ang hui kuan dan.) 我想兑现这张汇款单。

Let's
speak
phrasebook
of mandarin
Chinese

PART 8

* banknote	chāopiào (chow pee-ow)	钞票
* cash	xiànjīn (she-an gin)	现金
* small change	língqián (ling chee-an)	零钱
* coin	yìngbì (ying bee)	硬币

9. I would like to change these dollars to RMB.

Wǒ xiǎng bǎ zhèxiē měiyuán duìhuàn chéng rénmínbì. (Wuh she-ang ba juh she-ay may you-an 'd'-way huan chung ren min bee.)

我想把这些美元兑换成人民币。

10. What's the (country - ex. US) exchange rate today?

Jīntiān de měiguó huìlǜ shì duōshao? (Gin tee-an duh may go-uh hui lü sure doh-uh sh-ow?)

今天的美国汇率是多少？

11. I lost my card. I want to report it.

Wǒ de kǎ diū le, wǒ yào guàshī. (Wuh duh ka dee-oh luh, wuh yow guah sure.) 我的卡丢了，我要挂失。

12. I want to close this account.

Wǒ xiǎng qǔxiāo zhège zhànghù. (Wuh she-ang chew she-ow juh guh 'j'-ang who.) 我想取消这个账户。

13. Please tell me my balance.

Qǐng gàosù wǒ zhànghù yú'é. (Ching gow sue wuh 'j'-ang who yoo are.) 请告诉我账户余额。

14. Can I use my credit card here?

Wǒ de xìnyòngkǎ zài zhèr néng yòng ma? (Wuh duh shin yong ka 'tz'-eye jur neng yong ma?) 我的信用卡在这儿能用吗？

15. Can I withdraw some money from this cash machine?

Wǒ de xìnyòngkǎ néng zài tíkuǎnjī shang qǔ qián ma? (Wuh duh shin yong ka neng 'tz'-eye tee kuan gee shang chew chee-an ma?) 我的信用卡能在提款机上取钱吗？

Using a Telephone
Dǎ Diànhuà (Da Dee-an Hwa) 打电话

1. Is there a ... nearby?

Fùjìn yǒu ... ma? (Foo gin yoh ... ma?) 附近有 ... 吗？

* telephone booth
  diànhuàtíng (dee-an hwa ting) 电话亭
* public telephone
  gōngyòng diànhuà (gong yong dee-an hwa) 公用电话

外国人说中国话

Let's
speak
phrasebook
of mandarin
Chinese

PART 8

2. I have to put through a ...(call) to ...

wǒ yào gěi ... dǎ ge ... (diànhuà).

(Wuh yow gay ... da guh ... (dee-an hwa).)

我要给 ... 打个 ...（电话）。

* direct dial call
  zhíbō diànhuà (jur boh-uh dee-an hwa) 直拨电话
* long distance call
  chángtú diànhuà (chang too dee-an hwa) 长途电话
* collect call
  duìfāng fù fèi diànhuà ('d'-way fong foo fay dee-an hwa)
  对方付费电话
* coin call
  tóu bì diànhuà (toe bee dee-an hwa) 投币电话
* local call
  shì nèi diànhuà (sure nay dee-an hwa) 市内电话

3. Who would you like to speak to?

Qǐng wèn nín zhǎo shuí? (Ching when nin 'j'-ow 'sh'-way?) 请问您找谁？

Who would you like to speak to?
Qǐng wèn nín zhǎo shuí?

4. Who shall I say is calling, sir?

Qǐng wèn guìxìng, xiānsheng? (Ching when 'g'way shing, she-an sheng?) 请问贵姓，先生？

5. Please hold a moment.

Qǐng shāo děng. (Ching sh-ow deng.) 请稍等。

6. Sorry, you've dialed the wrong number.

Duìbuqǐ, nín dǎ cuò le. ('d'way boo chee, nin da 'ts'-oh-uh luh.) 对不起，您打错了。

7. How much per minute?

Yī fēnzhōng duōshao qián? ('e' fen zhong doh-uh show chee-an?) 一分钟多少钱？

8. What's your ...?

Nǐ de ... shì duōshao? (Knee duh ... sure doh-uh show?) 你的 ... 是多少？

---

* country number
  guójiā qū hào (go-uh gee-ah chew how) 国家区号
* city number
  chéngshì qū hào (chung sure chew how) 城市区号
* district number
  qū hào (chew how) 区号
* telephone number
  diànhuà hàomǎ (dee-an hwa how ma) 电话号码
* mobile phone number

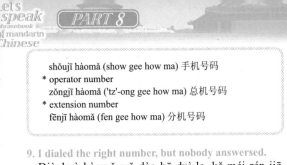

shǒujī hàomǎ (show gee how ma) 手机号码

* operator number
zǒngjī hàomǎ ('tz'-ong gee how ma) 总机号码

* extension number
fēnjī hàomǎ (fen gee how ma) 分机号码

9. I dialed the right number, but nobody answered.

Diànhuà hàomǎ wǒ dào bō duì le, kě méi rén jiē.
(Dee-an hwa how ma wuh dow boh-uh 's' way luh,
kuh may ren gee-ay.)
电话号码我倒拨对了，可没人接。

At the Hospital
Zài Yīyuàn ('tz'-eye 'e' You-an) 在医院

1. I feel bad today.

Wǒ jīntiān gǎnjué bù shūfú. (Wuh gin tee-an gan
jew-ay boo shoe foo.) 我今天感觉不舒服。

2. I've got a cold.

Wǒ gǎnmào le. (Wuh gan mao luh.) 我感冒了。

3. I'm running a high fever and feeling terrible.

Wǒ fā gāoshāo, gǎnjué zāo tòu le.
(Wuh fah gow sh-ow, gan jew-ay tzow toe luh.)

我发高烧，感觉糟透了。

4. I have a bad headache and a sore throat.

Wǒ de tóu téng de lìhài, sǎngzi yě téng.
(Wuh duh toe teng duh lee hi, sang 'tz'-uh yeh teng.)
我的头疼得厉害，嗓子也疼。

5. The pain has increased in intensity.

Téngtòng yuè lái yuè jùliè. (Teng tong you-eh lie you-eh jew lee-ay.) 疼痛越来越剧烈。

Symptoms Zhèng Zhuàng (Jung Jee-ang) 症状

* pain
  téng (teng) 疼
* dizzy
  yūn (yun) 晕
* swollen
  zhǒng (zhong) 肿
* nausea
  ěxīn (are shin) 恶心
* vomiting
  ǒutù (oh too) 呕吐
* itchy
  yǎng (yang) 痒
* weak
  xūruò (shoe roe-uh) 虚弱

* feeble
  wúlì (woo lee) 无力
* tired
  píláo (pee low) 疲劳
* blood
  líuxuè (lee-oh shoe-ay) 流血
* burn
  shāoshāng (sh-ow shang) 烧伤
* scald
  tàngshāng (tang shang) 烫伤
* cramp
  chōujīn (choh gin) 抽筋
* cough
  késou (kuh so) 咳嗽
* diarrhea

PART 8

Let's
speak
phrasebook
of mandarin
Chinese

fùxiè (foo shoe) 腹泻
* bellyache
fù tòng (foo tong) 腹痛
* cold
gǎnmào (gan mao) 感冒
* fever
fāshāo (fah sh-ow) 发烧
* allergic
guòmǐn (go-uh min) 过敏
* insomnia
shīmián (sure me-an) 失眠
* infection
chuánrǎn (chew-an ran) 传染
* faint
hūn dǎo (hun dow) 昏倒
* coma
hūnmí (hun me) 昏迷
* high blood pressure
gāoxuèyā (gao shoe-ay yah) 高血压
* drowsy
hūn hūn yù shuì (hun hun you 'sh'-way) 昏昏欲睡
* lack of appetite
shíyù bù zhèn (sure you boo jen) 食欲不振

6. He suffered serious injuries to ...

Tā de ... yánzhòng shòushāng.

(Ta duh ... yan zhong show shang.)

他的 ... 严重受伤。

7. His problem is quite serious. So he has to be hospitalized.

Tā bìng de bǐjiào yánzhòng, zhǐ néng zhùyuàn.

(Ta bing duh bee gee-ow yan zhong, jur neng jew you-an.) 他病得比较严重，只能住院。

8. Is my illness serious?

Wǒ de bìng yánzhòng ma?

(Wuh duh bing yan zhong ma?)

我的病严重吗？

9. Nurse, I would like an injection.

Hùshi, wǒ dǎzhēn. (Who sure, wuh da jen.)

护士，我打针。

Body Part Shēntǐ Bùwèi (Shen Tee Boo Way) 身体部位

* head	tóu (toe) 头	
* eye	yǎnjing (yan jing) 眼睛	
* ear	ěrduo (are doh-uh) 耳朵	
* nose	bízi (bee 'tz'-uh) 鼻子	
* mouth	zuǐ ('tz'-way) 嘴	
* teeth	yáchǐ (yah chur) 牙齿	
* throat	yānhóu (yan hou) 咽喉	
* neck	jǐng bù (jing boo) 颈部	
* shoulder	jiānbǎng (gee-an bang) 肩膀	
* back	hòu bèi (hou bay) 后背	

外国人说中国话

* chest	xiōng bù (she-ong boo)	胸部
* heart	xīnzàng (shin 'j'-ang)	心脏
* stomach	wèi (way)	胃
* arm	gēbo (guh boh-uh)	胳膊
* hand	shǒu (show)	手
* finger	shǒuzhǐ (show jur)	手指
* leg	tuǐ (too-ay)	腿
* knee	xīgài (she guy)	膝盖
* foot	jiǎo (gee-ow)	脚

10. Which department should I register with?

Wǒ yīnggāi guà nǎge kē? (Wuh ying guy guah na guh kuh?) 我应该挂哪个科?

Department Kē (Kuh) 科

* medical department
  nèikē (nay kuh) 内科
* surgical department
  wàikē (why kuh) 外科
* pediatrics
  ér kē (are kuh) 儿科
* cardiology
  xīnzàng kē (shin 'tz'-ang kuh) 心脏科
* dentistry
  yá kē (yah kuh) 牙科
* orthopedics
  gǔ kē (goo kuh) 骨科

11. Take the medicine three times a day.

Měi tiān sān cì, ànshí chī yào. (May tee-an san 'ts'-uh, an sure chur yow.) 每天三次，按时吃药。

---

* doctor
  yīshēng ('e' sheng) 医生
* precription
  chǔfāng (chew fong) 处方
* emergency room
  jízhěn shì (gee jen sure) 急诊室
* operating room
  shǒushù shì (show shoe sure) 手术室
* ward
  bìng fáng (bing fong) 病房
* pharmacy
  yàofáng (yow fong) 药房

At the Barbershop & Beauty Salon
Lǐfà hé Měiróng (Lee Fah Huh May Rong)
理发和美容

1. I need a haircut.

Wǒ yào lǐfà. (Wuh yow lee fah.) 我要理发。

---

2. How much do you charge for …?

… yào duōshao qián?
(… yow doh-uh sh-ow chee-an?) … 要多少钱？

外国人学说中国话

3. Just a trim, and cut the ... short, but not so much at the ....

Xiūjiǎn yī xià jiù xíng le. ... jiǎn duǎn xiē, dàn ... bù yào jiǎn de tài duō. (She-oh gee-an 'e' she-ah gee-oh shing luh. ... gee-an do-an shoe, dan ... boo yow gee-an duh tye doh-uh.) 修剪一下就行了。... 剪短些, 但 ... 不要剪得太多。

---

* back-side	hòumiàn (hou me-an)	后面
* front-side	qiánmiàn (chee-an me-an)	前面
* top	shàngmiàn (shang me-an)	上面
* sides	cèmiàn ('ts'-uh me-an)	侧面
* bang	liúhǎi (lee-oh hi)	刘海
* temples	bìnjiǎo (bin gee-ow)	鬓角
* shave	xiūmiàn (shoe me-an)	修面

---

4. I want to have a..., please.

Wǒ xiǎng ... (Wuh she-ang ...) 我想 ...

---

* shampoo
  xǐ tóu (she toe) 洗头
* facial
  miàn bù měiróng (me-an boo may rong)
  面部美容
* facial massage
  zuò liǎn bù ànmó ('z'-oh-uh lee-an boo an moh-uh)
  做脸部按摩

---

* cutting & styling
  zuò fàxíng ('z'-oh-uh fah shing) 做发型
* permanent wave
  tàngfà (tang fah) 烫发
* hair-dyeing
  rǎn fà (ran fah) 染发
* shampoo
  xǐ fà (she fah) 洗发
* beauty treatment
  měiróng (may roong) 美容
* manicure
  xiū zhǐjia (shoe jur gee-ah) 修指甲
* nutritious
  zīyǎng ('tz'-uh yang) 滋养
* repair
  xiū hù (shoe who) 修护

5. **I'd like to dye my hair wine red.**

Wǒ xiǎng bǎ tóufà rǎn chéng jiǔhóngsè.
(Wuh she-ang ba toe fah ran chung gee-oh hong suh.)
我想把头发染成酒红色。

6. **Your hair dryer is too hot.**

Diàn chuīfēng tài rè le. (Dee-an chuh-way feng tye
ruh luh.) 电吹风太热了。

7. **Please trim my eyebrows and darken them.**

Qǐng bǎ méimao xiū yī xià, zài huà shēn yīdiǎnr.

(Ching ba may mao shoe 'e' she-ah, 'tz'-eye hwa shen 'e' dee-an.) 请把眉毛修一下，再画深一点儿。

---

8. What kind of hair style would you like?

Nǐ xiǎng yào jiǎn shénme yàng de fàxíng?
(Knee she-ang yow chee-an shen muh yang duh fah shing?) 你想要剪什么样的发型？

Just a trim
Xiūjiǎn yī xià jiù xíng le.

I'd like to dye my hair wine red.
Wǒ xiǎng bǎ tóufà rǎn chéng jiǔhóngsè.

Hairdo	Fàxíng	(Fah Shing) 发型

* thinning   xiāo báo (shoe-ay bow) 削薄
* crop   píngtóu (ping toe) 平头
* part hair   fēn fà (fen fah) 分发
* long hair   cháng fà (chang fah) 长发
* short hair   duǎn fà (do-an fah) 短发
* straight hair   zhí fà (jur fah) 直发

* curly hair   juǎn fà (jew-an fah) 卷发
* bald head   guāngtóu ('g'wang tou) 光头

Photography
Shèyǐng (Shuh Ying) 摄影

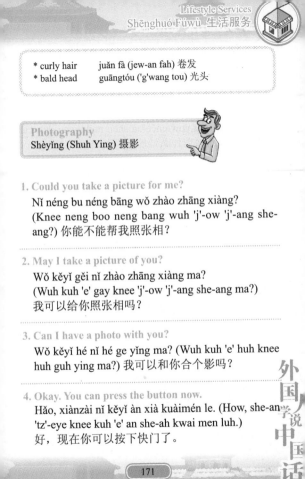

1. **Could you take a picture for me?**

   Nǐ néng bu néng bāng wǒ zhào zhāng xiàng?
   (Knee neng boo neng bang wuh 'j'-ow 'j'-ang she-ang?) 你能不能帮我照张相？

2. **May I take a picture of you?**

   Wǒ kěyǐ gěi nǐ zhào zhāng xiàng ma?
   (Wuh kuh 'e' gay knee 'j'-ow 'j'-ang she-ang ma?) 我可以给你照张相吗？

3. **Can I have a photo with you?**

   Wǒ kěyǐ hé nǐ hé ge yǐng ma? (Wuh kuh 'e' huh knee huh guh ying ma?) 我可以和你合个影吗？

4. **Okay. You can press the button now.**

   Hǎo, xiànzài nǐ kěyǐ àn xià kuàimén le. (How, she-an 'tz'-eye knee kuh 'e' an she-ah kwai men luh.) 好，现在你可以按下快门了。

外国人学说中国话

Let's
speak
Phrasebook
of Mandarin
Chinese

PART 8

5. Say "cheese"!

Shuō "qiézi"! (Show-uh "chee-ay 'tz'-uh"!)

说 "茄子" ！

---

6. You are very photogenic.

Nǐ fēicháng shàngxiàng.

(Knee fay chang shang she-ang.)

你非常上相。

---

7. Can you have this roll of film developed and printed?

Qǐng bǎ zhè juǎn jiāojuǎn chōngxǐ yī xià, kěyǐ ma?

(Ching ba juh jew-an gee-ow jew-an chong she 'e' she-ah, kuh 'e' ma?)

请把这卷胶卷冲洗一下，可以吗？

---

8. I want to enlarge this photograph.

Wǒ xiǎng fàngdà zhè zhāng zhàopiānr.

(Wuh she-ang fong da juh 'j'-ang 'j'-ow pee-an.)

我想放大这张照片儿。

---

9. Will my film be processed the day after tomorrow?

Wǒ de jiāojuǎn hòutiān kěyǐ chōngxǐ chūlái ma?

(Wuh duh gee-ow jew-an hou tee-an kuh 'e' chong she chew lie ma?)

我的胶卷后天可以冲洗出来吗？

* photo studio
  zhàoxiàng guǎn ('j'-ow she-ang gu-on) 照相馆
* digital camera
  shùmǎxiàngjī (shoe ma she-ang gee) 数码相机
* memory card
  cúnchǔ kǎ ('ts'-un chew ka) 存储卡
* battery
  diànchí (dee-an chur) 电池
* rechargeable battery
  chōngdiàn diànchí (chong dee-an dee-an chur) 充电电池
* video camera
  shèxiàngjī (shuh she-ang gee) 摄像机
* flash
  shǎnguāngdēng (shan 'g'wang deng) 闪光灯
* film
  jiāojuǎn (gee-ow jew-an) 胶卷
* negative
  dǐpiàn (dee pee-an) 底片
* CD
  guāngpán ('g'wang pan) 光盘
* album
  xiàngcè (she-ang 'ts'-uh) 相册
* process
  chōngxǐ (chong she) 冲洗
* enlarge
  fàngdà (fong da) 放大

外国人说中国话

Appendix Fùlù (Foo Lu) 附录

> ## Major Tourist Destinations in Beijing
> Běijīng Shì Zhǔyào Lǚyóu Jǐngdiǎn (Bay Jing Sure Joe-uh Yow Lü Yoh Jing Dee-an)
> 北京市主要旅游景点

* The Great Wall
  Chángchéng (chang chung) 长城
* The Palace Museum (or Forbidden City)
  Gùgōng Bówòyuàn (Zǐ Jìn Chéng)
  (goo gong boh-uh woo you-an <'tz'-uh gin chung>）
  故宫博物院（紫禁城）
* The Summer Palace
  Yíhéyuán ('e' huh you-an) 颐和园
* The Temple of Heaven
  Tiāntán (tee-an tan) 天坛
* The Ming Tombs
  Míngshísānlíng (ming sure san ling) 明十三陵
* Tian'anmen Square
  Tiānānmén Guǎngchǎng
  (tee-an an men 'g'wang chang) 天安门广场
* The Lama Temple
  Yōnghégōng (yong huh gong) 雍和宫
* Peking Man Site at Zhoukoudian
  Zhōukǒudiàn Běijīng Yuánrén Yízhǐ
  (joe koh dee-an bay jing you-an ren 'e' jur)
  周口店北京猿人遗址

174

* Beihai Park
  Běihǎi Gōngyuán (bay hi gong you-an) 北海公园
* Prince Gong's Residence
  Gōngwángfǔ (gong wang foo) 恭王府
* The Old Summer Palace
  Yuánmíngyuán (you-an ming you-an) 圆明园
* Fragrant Hill Park
  Xiāngshān Gōngyuán (she-ang shan gong you-an)
  香山公园
* The Beijing Botanical Garden
  Běijīng Zhíwùyuán (bay jing jur woo you-an)
  北京植物园
* Longqing Gorge
  Lóngqìngxiá (long ching she-ah) 龙庆峡

Chinese Traditional Festivals
Zhōngguó Chuántǒng Jiéqìng (Zhong Go-uh Chew-an Tong Gee-ay Ching) 中国传统节庆

1. Spring Festival
   (the 1st day of the 1st lunar month)
   Chūnjié (Chun Gee-ay) 春节

---

* boiled dumplings
  jiǎozi (gee-ow 'tz'-uh) 饺子
* temple fair
  miàohuì (meow hui) 庙会
* firecrackers
  biānpào (bee-an pow) 鞭炮

* Spring Festival couplets
  chūnlián (chun lee-an) 春联

2. Lantern Festival
(the 15th day of the 1st lunar month)
Yuánxiāo Jié (You-an She-ow Gee-ay) 元宵节

* full-moon dumpling
  yuánxiāo (you-an she-ow) 元宵
* festive lantern
  huādēng (hwa deng) 花灯

3. Dragon Boat Festival
(the 5th day of the 5th lunar month)
Duānwǔ Jié (Do-an Woo Gee-ay) 端午节

* rice dumpling
  zòngzi ('tz'-ong 'tz'-uh) 粽子
* dragon-boat race
  sài lóngzhōu (sigh long joe) 赛龙舟

4. Mid-Autumn Festival
(the 15th day of the 8th lunar month)
Zhōngqiū Jié (Zhong Chee-oh Gee-ay) 中秋节

* family reunion
  tuányuán (too-an you-an) 团圆
* moon-cake
  yuèbing (you-eh bing) 月饼

5. Double-Ninth Festival
(the 9th day of the 9th lunar month)
Chóngyáng Jié (Chong Yang Gee-ay) 重阳节

* hiking
  dēnggāo (deng gow) 登高
* chrysanthemum wine
  júhuā jiǔ (jew hwa gee-oh) 菊花酒
* double-ninth cakes
  chóngyáng gāo (chong yang gow) 重阳糕

Animal of Chinese Zodiac
Shíèr Shēngxiào
(Sure Are Sheng She-ow) 十二生肖

* mouse
  shǔ (shoe) 鼠
* ox
  niú (knee-oh) 牛
* tiger
  hǔ (hoo) 虎
* rabbit
  tù (too) 兔
* dragon
  lóng (long) 龙
* snake
  shé (shuh) 蛇

* horse
  mǎ (ma) 马
* sheep
  yáng (yang) 羊
* monkey
  hóu (hou) 猴
* cock
  jī (gee) 鸡
* dog
  gǒu (goh) 狗
* pig
  zhū (joe-uh) 猪

Romanization
Luómǎ Pīnyīn (Low-uh Ma Pin Yin)
罗马拼音

a	jie (gee-ay)
ai (eye)	qie (chee-ay)
an	jian (gee-an)
ang	qian (chee-an)
ao (ow)	zhi (jur)
zha (zhah)	chi (chur)
cha (chah)	jin (gin)
zhai ('j'-eye)	qin (chin)
chai ('ch'-eye)	jing
zhan (jan)	qing (ching)
chan	jiu (gee-oh)
zhang ('j'-ang)	qiu (chee-oh)
chang	jiong (gee-ong)
zhao ('j'-ow)	qiong (chee-ong)
chao (chow)	zhuo (joe-uh)
zhe (juh)	chuo (choh-uh)
che (chuh)	zhou (joe)
zhen (jen)	chou (choh)
chen	zhu (jew)
zheng (jung)	chu (chew)
cheng (chung)	ju (jew)
ji (gee)	qu (chew)
qi (chee)	zhua (jew-ah)
jia (gee-ah)	zhuai (jew-eye)
qia (chee-ah)	chuai (chew-eye)
jiang (gee-ang)	zhuan (jew-an)
qiang (chee-ang)	chuan (chew-an)
jiao (gee-ow)	juan (jew-an)
qiao (chee-ow)	quan (chew-an)

zhuang (jee-ang)
chuang (chew-ang)
jue (jew-ay)
que (chew-ay)
zhui (juh-way)
chui (chuh-way)
zhun (jun)
chun
jun
qun (chun)
zhong
chong
en
er (are)
fa (fah)
fan
fang (fong)
fei (fay)
fen
feng
fo (foh-uh)
fou (foh)
fu (foo)
ha
hai (hi)
han
hang (hong)
hao (how)
hei (hay)
hen
heng
he (huh)
hou (hoh)
xi (she)

xia (she-ah)
xiang (she-ang)
xiao (she-ow)
xie (she-ay)
xian (she-an)
xin (shin)
xing (shing)
xiu (she-oh)
xiong (she-ong)
xu (shoe)
xuan (shoe-an)
xue (shoe-ay)
xun (sh-une)
hu (who)
hua (hwa)
huai (h-why)
huan
huang
hui
hun
hong
huo
yi ('e')
ran
rang
rao (row)
re (ruh)
ren
reng
ri (ree)
ruo (row-uh)
rou (row)
ru (roo)
ruan (roo-an)

rui (roo-'e')	kun ('k'uhn)
run	gong
rong	kong
ga	guo (go-uh)
ka	kuo (koh-uh)
gai (guy)	la
kai ('k'-eye)	lai (lie)
gan	lan
kan (can)	lang
gang	lao (low)
kang	le (luh)
gao (gow)	lei (lay)
kao (cow)	leng
gen	li (lee)
ken	liang (lee-ang)
geng	liao (lee-ow)
keng	lie (lee-ay)
ge (guh)	lian (lee-an)
ke (kuh)	lin
gou (goh)	ling
kou (koh)	liu (lee-oh)
gu (goo)	luo (low-uh)
ku (koo)	lou (low)
gua (guah)	lu
kua (kuah)	lü
guai (gu-eye)	luan
kuai (kwai)	lue (lu-ay)
guan (gu-on)	lun
kuan	long
guang ('g'wang)	ma
kuang ('qu'-ang)	mai (my)
gui ('g'way)	man
kui ('k'way)	mang
gun ('g' uhn)	mao

mei (may)	nue (new-ay)
men	nong
meng	e (uh)
mi (me)	ou (oh)
miao (meow)	ba
mie (me-eh)	pa
mian (me-an)	bai (buy)
min	pai (pie)
ming	ban
miu (me-oh)	pan
mo (moh-uh)	bang
mou (moh)	pang
mu (moo)	bao (bow)
na	pao (p-ow)
nai ('n'eye)	bei (bay)
nan	pei (pay)
nang	ben
nao (now)	pen
nei (nay)	beng
nen	peng
neng	bi (bee)
ni (knee)	pi (pee)
niang (knee-ang)	biao (bee-ow)
niao (knee-ow)	piao (pee-ow)
nie (knee-ay)	bie (bee-eh)
nian (knee-an)	pie (pee-eh)
nin	bian (bee-an)
ning	pian (pee-an)
niu (knee-oh)	bin
nuo (noah)	pin
nou (know)	bing
nu (new)	ping
nü	bo (boh-uh)
nuan (new-an)	po (poh-uh)

pou (poh)	sui (sway)
bu (boo)	sun
pu (poo)	song
sa (sah)	da
sai (sigh)	ta
san	dai (die)
sang	tai (tye)
sao (sow)	dan
se (suh)	tan
sen	dang
seng	tang
sha	dao (dow)
shai (sh-eye)	tao (tow)
shan	de (duh)
shang	te (tuh)
shao (sh-ow)	deng
she (shuh)	teng
shen	di (dee)
sheng	ti (tee)
shi (sure)	diao (dee-ow)
shou (show)	tiao (tee-ow)
shu (shoe)	die (dee-eh)
shua (shoe-ah)	tie (tee-eh)
shuai ('sh'-why)	dian (dee-an)
shuan (shoe-an)	tian (tee-an)
shuang (shoe-ang)	ding
shui ('sh'-way)	ting
shun	diu (dee-oh)
shuo (show-uh)	duo (doh-uh)
suo (sew-uh)	tuo (toh-uh)
sou (so)	dou (doe)
si	tou (toe)
su (sue)	du (do)
suan (sue-an)	tu (too)

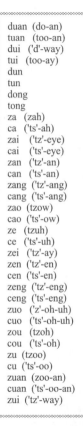

duan (do-an)	cui ('ts'-way)
tuan (too-an)	zun ('tz'-un)
dui ('d'-way)	cun ('ts'-un)
tui (too-ay)	zong ('tz'-ong)
dun	cong ('ts'-ong)
tun	zi ('tz'-uh)
dong	ci ('ts'-uh)
tong	wa (wah)
za (zah)	wai (why)
ca ('ts'-ah)	wan
zai ('tz'-eye)	wang
cai ('ts'-eye)	wei (way)
zan ('tz'-an)	wen (when)
can ('ts'-an)	weng
zang ('tz'-ang)	wo (wuh)
cang ('ts'-ang)	wu (woo)
zao (tzow)	ya (yah)
cao ('ts'-ow)	yai ('y'-eye)
ze (tzuh)	yang
ce ('ts'-uh)	yao (yow)
zei ('tz'-ay)	ye (yeh)
zen ('tz'-en)	yan
cen ('ts'-en)	yin
zeng ('tz'-eng)	ying
ceng ('ts'-eng)	yo (yoh)
zuo ('z'-oh-uh)	you (yoh)
cuo ('ts'-oh-uh)	yu (you)
zou (tzoh)	yuan (you-an)
cou ('ts'-oh)	yue (you-eh)
zu (tzoo)	yun
cu ('ts'-oo)	yong
zuan (zoo-an)	
cuan ('ts'-oo-an)	
zui ('tz'-way)	

Index

Let's *speak* phrasebook
Of mandarin *Chinese*

图书在版编目（CIP）数据

外国人学说中国话 / 旅舜主编.－北京：五洲传播出版社，2008.8
ISBN 978-7-5085-1388-1

Ⅰ.外... Ⅱ.旅... Ⅲ.汉语－口语－对外汉语教学－教材
Ⅳ.H195.4

中国版本图书馆CIP数据核字 (2008)第097130号

外国人学说中国话

Let's Speak – Phrasebook of Mandarin Chinese

主　编：旅舜		**Editor in Chief: Lü Shun**
责任编辑：侯明　王莉		**Managing Editor: Hou Ming Wang Li**
执行编辑：余泯然　赵伟玉		**Executive Editors: Yu Minran Zhao Weiyu**
装帧设计：帅芸		**Art Designer: Shuai Yun**
插　画：帅芸		**Illustrator: Shuai Yun**
语言顾问：Rick Reynolds		**Language Consultant: Rick Reynolds**

出版：五洲传播出版社
Published by: China Intercontinental Press
编者：北京精典博雅旅游图书有限公司
Edited by Beijing Jingdian Boya Traveling Book Co., Ltd
开本：889 × 1194 mm 64开
印张：3
印数：1-5000
版次：2008年8月第一版第一次印刷
书号：ISBN 978-7-5085-1388-1
http://www.旅游图书.cn　http://www.jdbybook.com

0004800
如发现质量问题，请致电 010-6711 8480 联系调换